The Calling of God

The Calling of God

Experiencing the Love of God in the Foundations of the Faith

Austin Reina

WIPF & STOCK · Eugene, Oregon

THE CALLING OF GOD
Experiencing the Love of God in the Foundations of the Faith

Wipf & Stock
An Imprint of Wipf and Stock Publishers
199 W. 8th Ave., Suite 3
Eugene, OR 97401

www.wipfandstock.com

PAPERBACK ISBN: 979-8-3852-3385-4
HARDCOVER ISBN: 979-8-3852-3386-1
EBOOK ISBN: 979-8-3852-3387-8

VERSION NUMBER 12/03/24

To Emmy and Gray,

In writing this work, I thought of you both often. I hoped that it may serve to further reveal the overwhelming, relentless, furious love of the Father, your heavenly Abba, your beloved daddy. My life's struggles, with successes and failures, have been in pursuit of this aim, but, no matter my efforts, I will always remain a pale display; I, then, pray that in writing it down I may at least provide for you a path to the all-enduring foundation, the love of your savior—seek him, remain there, and abide in his love. You know him, and he clearly has claimed you to be his own; there is nothing more than this, and, yet, he calls to you, "Further up, and further in."[1]

I love you always,

Your Daddy

1. Lewis, *Complete Chronicles of Narnia*, 520.

Everyone then who hears these words of mine and does them will be like a wise man who built his house on rock. And the rain fell, and the floods came, and the winds blew and beat on that house, but it did not fall, because it had been founded on the rock.

—Matt 7:24–25

Contents

Introduction

Before You Start

My hope and prayer for this endeavor is that it might serve merely as a tool to guide you in your walk with Christ. Just as Christ called his disciples to follow him,[2] to walk with him, to join in his adventure, the calling of God beckons us into an intentional relationship that plants our feet on solid ground. The aim of this study is to return to the foundations that we may stand firm as we are allured into further and further intimacy as his beloved disciples. This guide, however, cannot serve as a replacement for our personal encounters with Christ, our intimate and sincere relationships with the church, and our engagement with reading Scripture. On the contrary, the purpose of this conversation is to encourage us to pursue each of those facets deeper and with more understanding that we may continue to grow in our faith. As a fellow disciple struggling through this walk, the undeniable cry of my redeemed heart is to step further into the love of Christ. This is the calling on our lives, our hearts' pursuit: to grow in *intimacy* with Jesus and join the *fellowship* of the saints. Therefore, before we begin, let this be written upon your heart: intimacy and fellowship. Then, as you proceed through the following pages, do not let yourself worry about the amount of time it may or should take

2. Matt 4:19.

to get through it; to just get through it is not the point. It may be read quickly, of course, and I hope, if that is the case, that it will be a blessing to you. However, I want to encourage you to take your time. I am hoping and praying to call you to do more than simply read my ramblings—more importantly, read Scripture.

I've spent time in lecture halls deeply devouring details of Scripture and history, and I've sat in excitement during Bible scholar conferences during which academics brought to life the importance of what most consider to be minuscule details; but through it all, my desire is to read Scripture in the same manner as my wife's grandma. She is an amazing woman who has devoted her life to the gospel of Christ and to preaching boldly. And there are passages, most involving the crucifixion of Jesus, that she refuses to read before she goes to bed. She refuses to read them at that time because, instead of sleeping, she will otherwise spend her entire night weeping; for her, Scripture is alive with power and is far more than mere story. This is *information* deeply interwoven with *intimacy*. The difference in impact between scholarly reports and tear-stained Bibles is staggering—like the difference between reading informative junk mail versus a perfume laced letter from a lover. My prayer is that through this conversation we can begin to read Scripture with intimacy, knowledge, and tears.

Therefore, each section includes recommended Bible reading—a foundation for the conversation. This conversation will never amount to anything more than mere ramblings without the foundation of Scripture. Likewise, the focus of our devotions should be on Scripture with every other commentary merely serving as a minor tool, a guide, a companion. So, within each section, read the entire recommended book of the Bible. I understand that this will take longer; and, truly, it should take as much time as is needed. Can a time restraint be placed on improving our understanding of prayer? Or grace? Or the purpose of the church? It would be good to take whatever time is needed on whatever topic requires it—and, additionally, to not sit with those ponderings or prayers alone. It will be difficult to complete all the reading while also actively discussing it with others, but Christ is calling us to something challenging. Extremely difficult, but worthwhile. Truly, there is no other way, and nothing less will do—he deserves nothing less.

If this endeavor is beginning to sound intimidating, please remember that we do not pursue these efforts alone. If we did attempt the journey alone, we would quickly find our attempts fruitless. But again, we are not alone. As we seek to walk as disciples of Christ, we can hold fast to the promise of the presence and guidance of the Holy Spirit. Jesus told his disciples, "When the Spirit of truth comes, he will guide you into all the truth."[3] Without the Spirit, we cannot hope to begin to understand godly matters; with the help of the Holy Spirit, on the other hand, we can instead grow as knowledgeable and secure disciples. For "we have received not the spirit of the world, but the Spirit who is from God, that we might understand the things freely given us by God."[4]

We should also remember a few things along this journey . . .

Spend Time with Jesus

First, nothing is a replacement for time spent with Jesus. Each subject covered will include an encouraged prayer to simply get us started in our conversations with God. Let these scripted prayers act as a compass merely pointing the way; enjoy the path it leads us down, but as any good adventurer knows, the compass is only the beginning—continue the time with Jesus. Listen for his voice. Rest in his presence. Talk with the Father.

Spend Time with Believers

The next thing to remember is that we are not called to walk alone. In fact, we can't do it alone. We are called to "bear one another's

3. John 16:13.
4. 1 Cor 2:12.

burdens."[5] We are also told that it is not good for man to be alone;[6] this is not simply a reference to marriage (although it is that as well)—it's a call to relationship. We were created to have fellowship with the saints. Throughout this study, seek community. And, in this effort, it is recommended that we find two specific groups.

First, find people walking this journey and decide to walk it together. These small groups (outside of the Sunday morning gathering) are reflective of the example Christ set for us when he called his disciples. They had each other. They walked together, worked together, prayed together, ministered together, struggled together, and did life together. I encourage you, I implore you: find people with whom you can walk this out. Each section will include questions to ponder. Sit with them and consider them; but, more importantly, discuss them. Share openly within your small group and let it be a time of enlightenment and encouragement. While there is much we can do on our own, there is something special that happens when we are together. Again, this is not the same as being near each other—standing within a gathering is not the same as being in fellowship. We are to seek unity of heart, mind, and spirit in Christ. And, if you've never experienced this before, you'll find that the level of vulnerability required is outrageous. This is difficult, and most, instead, choose to avoid it. But to those brave enough . . .

The second thing I want to encourage you to find is a mentor. Find someone who has walked this journey for a while and found wisdom and maturity of faith. A mentor walks with you, guides you, shares stories of success and failure, and presents testimony to the faithfulness of God through many seasons of life. Another thing to remember is that one of the goals of this conversation is for us to grow in our faith and become a mentor to another. And we cannot truly become a mentor with faithful intent if we are unwilling to be mentored ourselves.

5. Gal 6:2.

6. Gen 2:18.

If you are struggling to find either a small group or a mentor, please reach out to the church, and I'm sure you'll be able to be connected to wonderful people.

Spend Time in God's Word

Lastly, this study is specifically designed to encourage us to dive into God's word. If you do not have a Bible, please make it a priority to ask first thing on Sunday morning—and I beg you to not leave the church building until you are holding a Bible in your hands! Many people can find themselves intimidated to read the Bible, and it can be for many different reasons. We may be intimidated by the length of it (it's a big book!). We may feel as though we are not equipped to understand what it is saying. We might feel as though it will be too convicting or as though we aren't worthy. The goal of this study is to give us the tools to better understand God's word, to read Scripture with confidence, and to write the words of God on our hearts.

Each section, each topic, will be primarily founded upon a book of the Bible; passages of Scripture from other parts of the Bible will be used, but there will be a particular book of the Bible recommended for each section. Also, throughout the conversation, verses of Scripture will be referenced, but we will be encouraged to read entire books of the Bible—for instance, we should read all of Proverbs, not just the parts we conveniently highlighted.

God did not give us the Bible as an unsolvable mystery to confuse or hinder us. That is one reason why it is also called "a light to my path."[7] The Bible is God revealing himself. He wants to be known; he wants to be known by you! This does not mean that we will, through simple reading, know all things; we are limited, and we all must grow in understanding, knowledge, and wisdom. Of course we will have questions, and some verses or teachings may take us longer to comprehend. Many things may take us our whole lives! And some things are worth spending our lives trying to comprehend. But we

7. Ps 119:105.

must not allow ourselves to be detoured from Scripture because we do not consider ourselves to be scholarly enough to comprehend it. The Bible is accessible. Also, because it is God's word given to us for the purpose of God revealing himself, it is also powerful. Reading Scripture will change you because his truth is living and real and sovereign. His truth is *the* truth. To make this very clear, this makes reading the Bible far more important than reading *about* the Bible. Both are good, but one is infinitely better.

Many people, whether they like to admit it or not, find themselves from time to time intimidated by the Bible. Most commonly, many believers don't know where to start. First and foremost, we must dispel the myth (or perhaps better stated: the lie) that the Bible is complicated. Historically, particularly in medieval times, there have unfortunately been many in positions of power who have encouraged this arrogant teaching to discourage believers from engaging Scripture. Why? Sadly, to maintain or increase their own power, influence, or status. They instead argued that they alone were capable of reading with understanding and that it was their duty to provide accurate interpretation. This was, in fact, the primary battleground of Martin Luther during the Reformation; he wanted to make the Bible, as opposed to commentaries from leadership, primary in the lives of believers. Still, this lie from so long ago has subconsciously lingered and is still present in the lives of so many. Beyond history, we must also know that we face a spiritual battle; the enemy does not want us to read Scripture—and the devil is a convincing liar. Therefore, let us put away bad teachings historically passed down from corrupt leaders and condemn the lies from hell. Here's the truth: you can read the Bible.

Practically speaking, there are steps that we can take to improve our enjoyment of reading Scripture and increase our understanding. First, read Scripture in context. Randomly picking verses out of context and attempting to find application is a frustrating path; and, it can lead to poor theology. Instead, try reading a book from beginning to end. This may be intimidating for some books of the Bible; but remember, some books are longer than others. Most books of the New Testament can be read in their entirety in an hour or less. Some books are even less than a page. Be encouraged! You can do this! And, while you are diving into Scripture, be sure to invite the presence of the Holy Spirit; again, the Spirit is your helper.[8] To read Scripture in the Spirit is to humbly and teachably request his guidance through your studies that you may obtain trust and wisdom.

Also, our approach to Scripture should build, like a staircase, upon simple principles: history, language, and application. In this approach, we are encouraged to:

1. gain understanding of the historical context of Scripture,
2. improve appreciation for the specificity of the language used throughout Scripture, and
3. seek interpretation and application based on the understanding of the two previous points.

This approach brings to life the relatable struggles that God's people have experienced and how God uses his word to meet his people where they are; without an understanding as to *what* Scripture is addressing, the message is hindered. Simply stated, we need to know what's going on. For example, the apostle Paul wrote many letters to various churches; knowing what is happening in that surrounding region or during that time or even within that church may help us understand what Paul is communicating. Why is Paul writing the letter in the first place? We know that all of the New Testament apostles were writing letters to various churches to address problems and encourage church members; the apostles were addressing specific problems including how to live out the Christian life during times of persecution, how to conduct church gatherings, and the need to avoid incorrect teachings. In order to understand the letters, we simply need to pay attention to what the letter is addressing, to whom the apostle is writing, and what is being said about the problem. Likewise, when trying to understand the prophets of the Old Testament we need to remember that they are always going to be giving God's message to a wayward people;

8. John 15:26.

these books are full of God's promises, but ultimately they were heading in the wrong direction, and God was calling them back to him. There are many different online tools or commentaries that we can reference to help us with this first step. Also, many study Bibles include some of this information at the beginning of each book. We do not need to be historians to complete this first step, but we do need to appreciate history. Second, this approach also emphasizes the need to read Scripture carefully and with specificity—words have meaning, and God chose them well. Throughout church history, loose understanding of the language used has often resulted in poor theology and dangerous application. Despite what our world has to say today, words have meaning. Then, only once we understand the context in which the Scripture was written and what it precisely states, can we accurately apply its message to our daily lives—and knowledge without application is foolishness; wisdom is knowledge in practice.

The Goal

Again, the goal of this conversation is to help us grow in our faith and help us find our foundations on nothing more than Christ Jesus; he is our solid rock. Through this conversation, we will walk from the importance of knowing God's word to the power of prayer, then from understanding our fallen and sinful condition to the gift of amazing grace because of the unchanging character of God. Next, we'll venture from the response of repentance to the devotion of living a life imitating Christ, then from becoming a disciple of Christ to engaging the church and spreading the good news of the gospel. Finally, we will focus on remembering the truth of Jesus and not letting ourselves be drawn away by a different gospel. Through it all, we will focus our attention on what has always mattered most. The most important commandment of the Bible, according to Jesus,[9] is found in Deuteronomy; we are

9. Mark 12:30.

called to love God with all of our being. Let this study help us in that effort.

> Hear, O Israel: The Lord our God, the Lord is one. You shall love the Lord your God with all your heart and with all your soul and with all your might. And these words that I command you today shall be on your heart. You shall teach them diligently to your children, and shall talk of them when you sit in your house, and when you walk by the way, and when you lie down, and when you rise. You shall bind them as a sign on your hand, and they shall be as frontlets between your eyes. You shall write them on the doorposts of your house and on your gates.[10]

10. Deut 6:4–9.

Lord,

I thank you for your grace, and I praise you for your goodness. Thank you for saving me and letting me be called a child of God. Thank you, Jesus, that salvation is only the beginning, and that you have promised even greater things as I follow you. Guide me, O Lord, as your disciple; I have chosen to follow you, and I want to know you more. And as I seek you, give me a passion for your word, and grant me the wisdom to understand your teachings. I want your word to be written on my heart that I may love you with all of my heart, all of my soul, and all of my mind. I love you, Lord, and I pray that I may grow in my knowledge of the depth of your unfathomable love.

Thank you for revealing yourself through your word that I may learn of your wonders and marvel at your renown. I praise you for being the same yesterday, today, and tomorrow; and I know all your promises are yes and amen. You are Lord above all. I am humbled, O Lord, at the wonder of your faithfulness. Give me wisdom, O God, and understanding, O Lord, that I may stand evermore in awe of you. Teach me your ways and help me, Jesus, to never part from them. I long to grow in knowledge, in righteousness, in understanding, and in awe of your greatness.

I pray this in the mighty name of Jesus.

Amen.

CHAPTER I

Talking to Jesus

Recommended Reading: Psalms

Deep within our hearts and psyche, woven into the very structure of our veins, is the desire for intimacy, a longing to connect. And, although many speak of spirituality as though it is a foggy otherness lacking clarity and tangibility, the longed-for connection that is the desperation of our hearts is truly available to us as something real and present. We were made for a *real* connection. However, our desperation will not be satisfied with meager relation; the cry of our souls is to find our place in the transcendent, the one beyond. We were carefully crafted by a loving creator, and, ever since, we have been anguished to return to the unwavering unity experienced in the garden. The great news is that the transcendent has made himself available, and he too seeks *real* union with ferocity. He wants to spend time with us. Many pastors and devotionals speak on the power of prayer and the need to hear from the Lord (and this is good), but prayer is first and foremost about intimacy. Through prayer we find *mutual* relationship with a God excited to lift us up, mend our hearts, fill our voids, and set us on a path of adventure. If this sounds over the top, read Psalms. As we begin our journey through the wild frontier that is being a disciple of Christ, there is no better place to start the conversation than with a study of prayer; through all the highs and lows of our humble walk with God, prayer will be essential. To begin simply, prayer is connecting with God—it's an ongoing conversation (not magic or mystery), and it's the conversation that our hearts have been desperately yearning for since our expulsion from the garden of Eden. So, again, to further understand prayer, we can turn to Psalms.

The book of Psalms is described as poetry and song, but, most importantly, it is a book of prayer. Through the book of Psalms we find prayers of thanksgiving, prayers of praise, prayers for deliverance, prayers for intercession, prayers of lament, prayers of petition, prayers of surrender, prayers of joy, prayers of meditation, and even prayers of anger. This, then, leads us to our first question: What is prayer? Again, simply stated, prayer is talking to Jesus. We are able, through divine grace and the goodness of God, to come before him, to spend time with him, to speak with him. Many people overcomplicate prayer, which can leave others intimidated; we'll talk about various forms of prayers, but, ultimately, we must remember that prayer is talking to Jesus.

As we are reading through the psalms, try to avoid reading them as mere poetry or even uplifting passages of Scripture. Psalms is full of God's promises and is often read as a great source of comfort and encouragement; but it can also be read as a collection of deep, heartfelt prayers. Then, we should also feel led to join the saints and let the psalms become our prayers!

The Purpose of Prayer

The purpose of prayer is to spend time with God. Through this time we pour out our hearts before God, express praise and adoration, and boldly declare his goodness. But it is also important to remember that prayer can be a time of listening. We often think of prayer as us speaking to God; but how often do we provide time for God to speak back? In any good conversation, there is a two-way dialogue. We speak, listen, share, and respond. It is the same with prayer. God is active and present; he also longs for union and intimacy. Unfortunately, many have made prayer about grandiose displays or so-called correct language instead of sincere intimacy. Prayer is not powerful because we speak the "right" words and dictate God's actions (that sounds like heresy and magic). The philosopher Martin Buber once addressed this exact question: "What distinguishes sacrifice and prayer from all magic?—Magic desires to obtain its effects without entering into relation."[1] Instead, prayer is powerful because through it we are connecting relationally with God Almighty, aligning our will to his, experiencing the movement of his spirit, and listening for his voice. Again, prayer is powerful because we are ushered into a real and mutual union with God. We must remember this point because the temptation is to have prayer focus entirely upon our needs and wants and not our connection to Christ or the stirrings of the Holy Spirit—even the great prophet Elijah mixed up his priorities from time to time, missing the opportunity for connection within moments of silence.

Moments of Silence

One of the great passages of Scripture that we hear about frequently concerns one of the most desperate moments in the life of Elijah.[2] However, the discussion is often told with a strong focus placed upon only a few verses with the intention of portraying the subtle displays of God's guiding voice; the preacher, ever so gently, whispers to the congregation that the booming voice depicted within well-known Charlton Heston films is not the presence that we are always granted. The preacher draws our attention ever closer by assuring us that, if we retreat into quiet solitude, we will begin to hear the whispers of the Father that desperately long to speak into our lives. It's a great message, and there is nothing incorrect about it. The story of Elijah depicts a beautiful but simple truth: if we will stop to listen, we will hear the whispers of a

1. Buber, *I and Thou*, 83.
2. 1 Kgs 19:9–15.

mighty God. Great preachers know the common temptation is for us to demand the booming voice and instead miss the still small voice beckoning us—alluring us—into his presence.

However, despite the great message of the common preaching, perhaps the epicenter of the passage should not be placed on the presence of the gentle whisper; rather, we should acknowledge that the passage is framed by the repetition of one particular question: "What are you doing here?"[3] Perhaps this question should draw far more of our attention.

Elijah, although he had recently summoned the fire of heaven upon a humble altar,[4] in addition to ending a famine by praying for the Lord's provision of rain[5]—quite possibly the most outstanding victories of his life—is running, in the very literal sense, for his life. The display of fire resulted in tremendous rage within the most wicked king to ever rule over God's people, and a sentence of death has been ordered for Elijah by King Ahab himself.[6] Elijah, upon hearing the news, retreated deep into the wilderness (to meet death on his own terms) where he was instead comforted by angelic messengers.[7] Once he finally regained his physical, emotional, and spiritual strength, he continued forward in his journey to search for the voice of God presumably to reconnect for his guidance.[8] However, once he finally begins to hear the long-awaited whispering voice, Elijah is not offered a message of guidance, comfort, or inspiration; instead, he is presented with a simple and rather peculiar question: "What are you doing here?"[9] Elijah's initial reaction, I suspect, was not too different than the one we would offer. He very clearly expresses the troubling events that need to be rectified.[10] We, likewise and understandably, approach our moments of silence with

3. 1 Kgs 19:9, 13.
4. 1 Kgs 18:20–40.
5. 1 Kgs 18:1–18, 41–46.
6. 1 Kgs 19:1–2.
7. 1 Kgs 19:3–5.
8. 1 Kgs 19:8.
9. 1 Kgs 19:9.
10. 1 Kgs 19:10.

the underlying motive of seeking a practical resolution to situations that are causing the most immediate anxiety within us. When we have troubles, we want answers; we think we need answers. As the narrative continues, we see that God does not respond as expected; his response to Elijah's list of troubles represents the second frame in the passage. God responds with the same question previously presented: "What are you doing here?"[11]

For most of us, this conversation likely spurs a basic response: "Why didn't he hear me the first time?" Instead of assuming that the repetition is significant, we assume that God must have misunderstood us—"Maybe God didn't hear me?" Because Elijah approached this peculiar reply with that very ignorance, he repeated his first speech; one might even imagine Elijah over-enunciating a slow-motion version of his previous concerns.[12] Although this is the common reaction that we all naively replicate, there are a few important questions: Does God have a hearing problem, or did Elijah not understand the depth of God's voice? Elijah doesn't even bother to rephrase his speech—instead, he implemented a strategy we, today, use all the time: copy and paste. Maybe God's question was supposed to be understood on a deeper level, but surely he must not know about my current struggles. Why would he, the Omniscient, ask such a question? What am I doing here? What answer was God originally hoping to receive from such a simple question? What answer would I give? What answer am I giving?

I often find that, in my own short-lived moments of silent solitude, listening for the depth of God's voice is the last thing on my mind. I struggle to quiet the internal voices that are rationally attempting to put together a biblically driven solution to a problem or set of problems. If I concentrate hard enough, if I quiet my mind enough, then maybe I'll be able to find my own solution. However, what this passage seems to suggest is that God is not as concerned with the small trials that we supposedly suffer daily as much as he is concerned with having our fully submitted attention. That is not to say that God doesn't care; after all, he

11. 1 Kgs 19:13.

12. 1 Kgs 19:14.

saw Elijah in the desert, and he sent the angel to care for him in his time of weakness. This *is* the same God that used the prophet Elisha to help a man find a borrowed axe head that got lost in the river.[13] The Bible is clear: he cares. But when we venture in search of the presence of God, the temptation is to place personal agenda above and beyond the priority it should be given: "God, here I am; now give me what I ask for!" The challenge, instead, is to humbly and with a sense of awe proclaim the words of Isaiah: "Here I am."[14] C. S. Lewis alludes to this very concept in his novel *Till We Have Faces* when the heroine reaches her enlightened conclusion that God *is* the answer: "I know now, Lord, why you utter no answer. You are yourself the answer. Before your face questions die away. What other answer would suffice?"[15]

In our moments of prayer, let us try starting with the assumption that God is asking us the very question he offered Elijah. Moreover, let's spend our prayers in an attempt to not follow the folly of Elijah's response. "But seek first the kingdom of God and his righteousness, and all these things will be added to you."[16]

"And the word of the LORD came to him: 'What are you doing here, Elijah?'"[17]

Moments of Prayer

Within our moments of prayer, there are various forms from which to approach the throne of God. We come before him formally, informally, and meditatively. Again, Scripture can be our guiding path.

Psalms is a great example of formal prayer. The authors spent time writing clear messages written in beautiful poetry. The writers of the psalms were specific in their words with their prayers

13. 2 Kgs 6:1–7.
14. Isa 6:8.
15. Lewis, *Till We Have Faces*, 308.
16. Matt 6:33.
17. 1 Kgs 19:9.

carefully crafted. This is a good thing. It is okay to prepare and plan your prayers. There is nothing wrong with formal prayer. In fact, formal prayer is typically more appropriate for public settings. Let's quickly state, however, that formal is not the same as pompous.

Within public settings, formal prayer shows a healthy consideration for the other people with whom we are praying. When our thoughts are organized and our message is clear, others are able to understand the heart and intention of our prayer allowing them to agree with us and join in the prayer (say "amen"). In this context, public formal prayer can edify the church and unite believers.

The danger of formal prayer can be found in losing sight of what matters most: the one to whom we are praying! In the Sermon on the Mount, Jesus warned us to avoid prayers that draw attention to ourselves;[18] these type of loud "fancy" prayers are designed to glorify the one who is praying. Formal prayer should not be confused with "fancy" prayer. Public prayer that is honoring to God, however, glorifies the Father. When praying in public, we should seek to glorify God in heaven, set our hearts upon him, pray with sincere honesty, and be considerate of those around us by making it easy for them to agree and join.

Beyond times of corporate prayer, the apostle Paul calls us to "pray without ceasing."[19] Throughout our day, in all our actions, in our comings and goings, through the chaos of life, through pain and sorrow, through joy and triumph, pray. Keep a running conversation with God. Consider for a moment that Christ calls us "friends."[20] If we spent the entire day with our best friend, the conversation would include many topics, and it would be constant. We would spend time listening and sharing. When spending the day with our best friend, we would share out loud the thoughts, questions, and concerns that we had in each moment. This is informal prayer. God wants to spend the entire day with you; he wants to be in conversation with you, and he cares about those small details in your life.

18. Matt 6:5.

19. 1 Thess 5:17.

20. John 15:15.

G. K. Chesterton was once asked in an interview what he would say if Jesus was standing right next to him; Chesterton responded that he is.[21] Chesterton knew and lived in the reality of the immediacy of God's presence, and this impacted the way he prayed. Long before Chesterton, Augustine wrote, "He who begot me and he who watches over me are one and the same, and for me there is no good but you, the Almighty, who are with me even before I am with you."[22] This is the power of ceaseless intimate prayers.

Also, Scripture encourages us to meditate upon the word.[23] Meditative prayer focuses on instilling God's truth in our hearts, speaking God's promises into our situations and experiences, and keeping our minds founded upon the Father. For example, author and preacher Brennan Manning encouraged many to pray a simple prayer: "Abba, I belong to you."[24] Abba, best translated as daddy, is the name under which Christ encourages us to pray,[25] and Manning instructs us to blend it with the truth of Song of Songs 2:16—"I am his." This simple prayer is powerful and profound; it will change the way we pray. Through such a basic prayer—the prayer of "I am his"—we discover the true beauty of the allegory presented in Song of Songs: we are the bride! And, far more than that, the bridegroom longs for us and claims us as his beloved.

Our prayer life should also be guided by Scripture. Again, Psalms is a great place to start. Read through Psalms. Meditate on the prayers of the saints that came before us. But, as said before, allow the Psalms to become your own prayers. Through this practice we'll find that our prayer life is deeply enriched with sound theology and the ever-present promises of God.

Beyond the book of Psalms, another book filled with beautiful, prayerful poetry is the Song of Songs. As a practice, try praying

21. Manning, *Abba's Child*, 79.

22. Augustine, *Confessions*, 210.

23. Ps 1:2; Josh 1:8; Ps 119:97.

24. Manning, *Furious Longing of God*, 46.

25. Matt 6:9.

passages such as "my beloved is mine, and I am his."[26] If you're daring enough, make the entire book your prayer; the voice of the bride would be your declarations before God, and the voice of the bridegroom is his response to you. And, if you've never read through Song of Songs, then, trust me, this is a challenge only for those daring enough to dive into profound, seductive intimacy. To such a challenge I implore you: be bold!

In the Sermon on the Mount, Jesus taught his disciples how to pray. It is a prayer that we all know well:

> Our Father in heaven, hallowed be your name.
>
> Your kingdom come.
>
> Your will be done, on earth as it is in heaven.
>
> Give us this day our daily bread.
>
> And forgive us our debts, as we also have forgiven our debtors.
>
> Lead us not into temptation, but deliver us from the evil one.[27]

Through this example, we are called to pray to our Father—the word used is Abba. And we are to praise his name, to keep his name holy. We are led to pray for the execution of the Father's will not only in our own lives but for the world as well. Then, we are encouraged to pray for "daily bread." The reference to daily bread is referring to the manna provided in the wilderness when God's people were completely dependent upon his provision; God wants us to be dependent upon him—in those times of dependency, we rely upon his will, his guidance, and his goodness. Jesus also instructs us to pray for forgiveness with an understanding that we are likewise called to forgive; this is a repeated instruction from Matt 5:23–24: "If you are offering your gift at the altar and there remember that your brother has something against you, leave your gift there before the altar and go. First be reconciled to your brother, and then come and offer your gift."[28] Lastly, we are

26. Song 2:16.

27. Matt 6:9–13.

28. Matt 5:23–24.

led to pray for God's continual deliverance from spiritual forces. The battle for our souls is real and there is one who, in his opposition to God, wants to "steal, kill, and destroy."[29] Despite what Hollywood might depict, the victory over the snares of the devil[30] will not come from our efforts; in fact, the battle is already won. Therefore, when we pray, we pray to the one who has conquered, the Christ given all authority.[31]

29. John 10:10.
30. 2 Tim 2:26.
31. Matt 28:18.

Questions to Ponder

1. Do you allow the shame of sin to keep you from praying?
2. In John 10:27, Jesus says, "My sheep know my voice." How much of your prayer life consists of listening to the voice of God?
3. What difficulties do you face when spending time in "listening prayer"?

Prayer

Abba, Father, I glorify your name! Let your name, the name above all names, be praised throughout the world. I pray that your will be done, O God, your ways be followed; I pray that all people will come to follow you just as you are followed and obeyed in heaven. I thank you, Jesus, for all that you have provided, and I pray that you will continue to provide and care for me as you have promised. Help me to stay far from temptation, to resist the false promises of sin; just as you delivered your people from slavery in Egypt, I know you have delivered me from the oppression of sin—hold me, Jesus, in your mighty arms; keep me from returning to my old ways. Forgive me, Father, for all the times I have disobeyed, for all the times I have sinned, for all the times I have chosen to return to my old ways (the way I lived before making you Lord *of my life). As you have forgiven me,* Lord, *I will continually forgive others when they do wrong against me, and I will not hold resentment against them for I know that when you forgive me you call me a friend. Amen.*

Abba, I belong to you.

CHAPTER 2

The Poor in Spirit

Recommended Reading: Romans, Genesis

If you want to watch people squirm, if you want to fight through every moment for your audience's attention, begin your presentation with the word sin. In fact, you might as well, as an obvious glutton for punishment, lavish on the pain by titling the message, "Sin: A Direct and Honest Conversation." Or, maybe even better, "You *Are* Worse Than You Think You Are." No one enjoys having to face the bitter reality that we are the poor in spirit, hopeless beggars, the sinful, and the fallen. A general audience will perk their ears to messages of grace and blessing, but, when confronted with sin, we fidget in our seats and allow our thoughts to shift toward other tasks and duties. The most humble ones drop their heads in shame and weep because they know their poverty and feel helpless in their position. But it was Christ who called the poor in spirit blessed.[1] This is not a conversation that we should avoid. As Philip Yancey said, "Any Greek scholar will tell you the word 'blessed' is far too sedate and beatific to carry the percussive force Jesus intended. The Greek word conveys something like a short cry of joy, 'Oh, you

1. Matt 5:3.

lucky person!' 'How lucky are the unlucky!' Jesus said in effect."[2] By diving into the deep, dark crevices of our hidden selves, we are able to stand in an alternate reality; shame gives way to blessing. Yancey continues, "With nowhere else to turn, the desperate just may turn to Jesus, the only one who can offer the deliverance they long for. Jesus really believed that a person who is poor in spirit, or mourning, or persecuted, or hungry and thirsty for righteousness has a peculiar 'advantage' over the rest of us."[3] The understanding of sin is vital to understanding Christianity. We must have a biblical perspective of sin and our fallen nature in order to understand so many other topics. Once we know and experience the depth of our fall from grace, we open our lives to the opportunity for blessing beyond compare. And there's no better place to start than the beginning. As we read Genesis, we should develop a few primary truths: we are created in the image of God, we are fallen and sinful, and God is ferociously pursuing us to restore our relationship with him. While reading Genesis, we can improve our grasp on what it means to be made in his image while also learning that there is a common thread in all sin; Genesis shows us what sin really is. But there is hope in restoration because we serve a God who desires to renew all things. "Human beings do not readily admit desperation. When they do, the kingdom of heaven draws near."[4] But again, let's start at the beginning . . .

Image Bearers

God created us to bear his image; we are created in the image of God. Although this is something that many of us have heard a thousand times before, it deserves repeating: "God created man in his image, in the image of God he created him; male and female he created them."[5] First and foremost, when understanding

2. Yancey, *Jesus I Never Knew*, 107.
3. Yancey, *Jesus I Never Knew*, 114.
4. Yancey, *Jesus I Never Knew*, 117.
5. Gen 1:27.

the nature of humanity, we must accept that we are created and endowed with a likeness of God. This is foundational and non-negotiable. Through this understanding we can know without a shadow of a doubt that life is precious, that we are set apart from the rest of creation, that we are not mere animals, and that human life has value. Also, that value is inherent—our value is not found in our achievements, usefulness, or capabilities. We have value because we were created by God, and we were created in the image of God. God did not create us in the same manner as everything else; we are different. In Psalms we also read, "You formed my inward parts; you knitted me together in my mother's womb."[6] We are not an accident; the Bible is clear in that we are carefully crafted by a loving God. Life, therefore, is precious, and we must protect it. But what does it mean to be created in his image? Through Genesis we can see the beauty and power of God that gives us a glimpse into who we were created to be.

First, God created. He is creative. He created us to be creative too. Again, this makes us different from the rest of nature; while apes may be able to finger paint smudges of colors on a canvas, there is no comparison to the expressions of art filling galleries all around the world. There are plenty of ways in which we see this creativity naturally within humanity, but the basics are the same. When given little, we can create symphonies and skyscrapers and even *creatively* problem-solve. Historically, among the first practices implemented by nihilists (those who believe that there is no meaning in life including no meaning to a person's existence) when assuming tyrannical political power is to remove individuality, art, and expression. Beautifully crafted architecture was chiseled down into square block houses; dull brown jumpsuits were issued as uniforms; art was confiscated. These regimes attempted to suppress God, and the inherent image of God, in the people's lives by drowning a basic display of our being created in his image. The result historically, by the way, was higher mortality rates, unfettered aggression, and despair.[7]

6. Ps 139:13.

7. Browning, *Ordinary Men*, 23–25; Frankl, *Man's Search for Meaning*,

Second, we can see that God did not simply create as though he was making random art for the mere sake of expression. God created order out of chaos. We serve a God of order. Through his beautiful creation, he created so much perfect order—laws of nature—that we can develop scientific methods by which to consistently study all that he has done. Again, there are many who seek to confuse and instill chaos, but in doing so they are forsaking the instilled image of God. This does not mean that we forgo moments of spontaneity, but we display the image of God when we create order out of chaos.

Sinners in Need of Salvation

Unfortunately, the story of Genesis does not continue where it began. At the very beginning, we quickly fell into sin. On this topic, there is an important point that must be understood. When speaking of sin, we are speaking both philosophically as well as practically—that is to say, we are speaking both of our nature as well as our deeds. Some teach that we are not, in the philosophical sense (within our nature), "fallen"; according to this teaching, we are born perfect but eventually succumb, inevitably, to sin. Theoretically (again, under this teaching), it is possible to live a perfect life if one could only take the right steps from the beginning. This, however, is not from the Bible. All of humanity, as an entire people (past, present and future), live outside of perfect communion with God. Apart from Christ, we exist under the curse of sin.[8] We cannot achieve perfection. We are, by nature, sinful. We are the poor in spirit,[9] beggars before the throne of God. We all need salvation. With this, we also must accept our sin nature according to our deeds; each one of us (fallen nature aside) have fallen short—everyone has sinned. We are not only born into a fallen nature; through the course of our lives we all

12–17; Newman, "Socialist Realism"; Sauytbay and Cavelius, *Chief Witness*, 33, 95, 105, 165; Solzhenitsyn, *Gulag Archipelago*, 5.

8. See Eph 2:3; 2 Pet 1:4; Col 2:11, 13; Rom 7:5, 25; 8:3.

9. Matt 5:3.

actively commit sinful deeds. To understand this clearly, we can turn to Paul's teachings in Romans.

In Romans, we read, "For all have sinned and fall short of the glory of God."[10] He continues, "Just as sin came into the world through one man, and death through sin, and so death spread to all men because all sinned."[11] And for any who believe that they have lived a sinless life, in the Sermon on the Mount Jesus equates insults with murder[12] and lust with adultery.[13] Clearly, the standards of heaven are far beyond ours. No one has lived a sinless life; we are the poor in spirit, beggars before the cross. We have nothing to offer even when at our best. According to Stassen, "The *poor in spirit* are those who find themselves waiting, empty-handed, upon God alone for their hope."[14] But this truth is not the end; again, we must remember that this uncomfortable, and often avoided, reality is called blessed by Christ. In 1847, Kierkegaard wrote, "How beautiful it is—that what betokens the deepest poverty likewise signifies the greatest riches! Need, to have need, and to be needy—how reluctantly a man wishes this to be said of him. . . . It is the religious man's highest and true wealth that he needs God."[15]

The Rebellion of Sin

To further understand our need for salvation, we need to better understand what sin is. In the garden of Eden, we read that there was only one rule: "The tree of the knowledge of good and evil you shall not eat, for in the day that you eat of it you shall surely die."[16] We might be tempted to believe that following a single rule should have been an easy task; but if we assume such a perspective we will miss the bewitching nature of sin. The temptation to disobey was

10. Rom 3:23.
11. Rom 5:12.
12. Matt 5:21–22.
13. Matt 5:27–30.
14. Stassen, *Living the Sermon*, 43.
15. Kierkegaard, *Works of Love*, 28.
16. Gen 2:17.

not found in the beauty or aroma of this tree's fruit; instead, the serpent tempts Eve with half truths:

> But the serpent said to the woman: "you will not surely die. For God knows that when you eat of it your eyes will be opened, and you will be like God, knowing good and evil." So when the woman saw that the tree was good for food, and that it was a delight to the eyes, and that the tree was to be desired to make one wise, she took of its fruit and ate.[17]

The temptation was to be like God, or, rather, to become a replacement for God. No, upon eating, Adam and Eve did not die an immediate physical death; but physical death came to them through old age along with the spiritual death of no longer being in perfect union with God. And, yes, we gained the divine knowledge of good and evil; however, in so doing we discovered that we were not capable of resisting evil and thereby became *less* like God. But what was our sin? What was the act that doomed all of humanity? An attempt to become God.

The debate as to which sin is more egregious, this or that, misses the foundation of what *sin* is: trying to be God. Why are all sins equal? How can Jesus justify a teaching equating insults with murder? Because all sin is our rebellious effort to be God. Sin occurs when we refuse the plans of God, ignore his instructions, and instead claim our perspectives and desires to be higher than his. Every sin is an attempted coup against the throne of God. We see these efforts continued in the story of the Tower of Babel[18] in which construction began on a building that reached the sky "to make a name for ourselves,"[19] to make a name that rivals God's.

When we understand that *all* sin is equal because *all* sin is treason against God, then, and only then, can we learn the need and capability to forgive others who have wronged us and the practice of not judging others.[20] With the proper understanding,

17. Gen 3:4–6.
18. Gen 11:1–9.
19. Gen 11:4.
20. Matt 7:1; Rom 14:13.

we learn to stop comparing our actions to the actions of others. I am a sinner. I am not better than you. You are a sinner; you are not better than me. No matter our list of sinful acts (which may differ between us), we find ourselves on equal ground at the same place: beggars at the merciful cross.

To be more specific, I should have said I *was* a sinner, but *now* I have been redeemed. More on that later . . .

Questions to Ponder

1. In what ways are you still rebelling?
2. How can your understanding of what sin truly is help you to not be judgmental?
3. In what ways can you live more fully into the image of God in your daily life?

Prayer

O Father,

I know I am a sinner. I know that I have not only been in the wrong and done what was wrong, but I also know that I am a broken, fallen, beggar before you. Thank you, O LORD, for your daily mercies. Thank you, Father, for your mercies are new every morning. Forgive me, God, according to your steadfast love and faithfulness. Keep me, Jesus, in your arms. Let me now be born of you and not keep on sinning.

Amen.

CHAPTER 3

To Know Christ

Recommended Reading: Gospel of John, Exodus

There are verses that we have all heard so many times that we begin to glance over them. Because we allowed ourselves to think that we can become overly familiar with certain information, certain passages of the Bible begin to feel uninteresting and are treated as though they are not as important. All of Scripture is the word of God, and in it is the intimate and powerful message of a loving, faithful God. However, there is one passage in particular that we could meditate on eternally and still stand in awe of and wonder at its beauty:

> For God so loved the world, that he gave his only Son, that whoever believes in him should not perish but have eternal life. For God did not send his Son into the world to condemn the world, but in order that the world might be saved through him.[1]

John knew, within all of his being, that Jesus loved him; John renamed himself "the one whom Jesus loved."[2] Others did not refer

1. John 3:16–17.
2. John 20:2.

to him as such, and there is no scriptural reference to indicate that Jesus loved John more than the others. But John knew Jesus loved him. He also very clearly understood the ministry of Jesus. He came that we might be saved through faith in him. And this salvation is by faith, our belief only in the work of Christ.[3] He has come to restore the relationship. These are simple verses that most children in Sunday school know by heart and, I hope, are told at every gathering; but as adults, we must hold fast to these couple sentences and let ourselves read them anew each and every day. This is the good news. This is the gospel. This is the medication that our hearts, souls, and minds desperately need. As we walk with Jesus, we must understand that without him the prognosis is far from bleak and way past dire. There are no other experimental treatment options that can be pursued or attempted; there's no amount of striving, struggling, or fighting that will make even a dent of an impact. We must know this. You, under your own efforts, are not pure enough to enter into the presence of a holy and perfect God. But John 3:16 speaks life to us; it is the hope we need. Because God loves you, he made a new covenant.

No Other Way

Under the old covenant, the holy presence of God was only experienced by the few who entered into the holy of holies. Within the tabernacle, the Spirit of God would descend and rest in the place called the holy of holies which also housed the ark of the covenant (the container for the Ten Commandments). Entrance beyond the veil that separated this room from the others was done under the strictest rituals with the requirement for perfect adherence to the law;[4] needless to say, the holy of holies was not available to any and all. However, as Christ died on the cross, the

3. Eph 2:8–9.

4. Lev 16; Exod 28:33–35.

veil in the temple was torn[5]—all that separated us from God was wiped clean by the blood of the Lamb.

Jesus states, "I am the way, and the truth, and the life. No one comes to the Father except through me."[6] There is no other way to the Father. There is no truth apart from *the* truth—Jesus. Without Jesus, there is no life because he *is* life. But this verse is also a direct reference to the tabernacle. There were three entrances to the holy of holies: the gate, the door, and the veil. Any seeking to enter the holy of holies must enter through these points. Jesus is the representation of these passages. If more convincing is needed, he even states, "I am the door."[7] Only through our trust in the saving work of Jesus can we find ourselves in union with God. And it is in response to this truth that Brennan Manning writes, "My deepest awareness of myself is that I am deeply loved by Jesus Christ and I have done nothing to earn it or deserve it."[8]

As you read through the Gospel of John, let yourself stand in awe, wonder, gratitude, and humility because reading the Gospel of John gives you direct insight into the heart of Jesus; John shows us the intimacy and passion of the one who came to give us eternal life with him.

No Longer Slaves

But the gospel message is not unique to the New Testament. God's truth and love are evident throughout Scripture. In fact, based on literary analysis, many scholars argue that the Exodus story was a major influence on the disciples—particularly Matthew. And, of course, it should be because not only was Moses considered by the Jewish people to be the chief prophet, but the Exodus story is also the story of salvation. Each year, the Jewish people celebrate the Passover as a reminder of when they were

5. Matt 27:51; Luke 23:45.
6. John 14:6.
7. John 10:9.
8. Manning, *Ragamuffin Gospel*, 11.

set free from their bondage in Egypt. Likewise, we were slaves to sin,[9] held captive under the oppression of sin, but Christ came that we may be set free; Jesus liberates us and delivers us. We are then, by the grace of God, led out of Egypt, out of our affliction, into a new land flowing with milk and honey.[10] The Hebrew people living in Egypt did nothing to deserve their deliverance; their deliverance is by the grace and love of God. When meeting with Moses through the burning bush, God tells Moses that he has been carefully watching his people with compassion; but, more than that, he is a God who takes action:

> I have surely seen the affliction of my people who are in Egypt and have heard their cry because of their taskmasters. I know their sufferings, and I have come down to deliver them.[11]

This famous story shows a God who opposes tyrannical empires and humbles any who would dare stand against him. Even the well-known plagues of Egypt are purposeful; each plague represents a direct challenge to specific Egyptian gods with the result being the same for each: there is only one God in heaven. God even says, "On all the gods of Egypt I will execute judgments."[12] Ultimately, Pharaoh is broken by the death of the firstborn. But the people of God were saved only by the covering of the blood of the lamb,[13] a lamb without blemish.[14] Then, having been set free, the people of God were given a new way to live; having been delivered from their affliction; God then gives them the Ten Commandments.[15] Adherence to the law did not bring God's salvation, and our attempt to adhere to the law will never result in our salvation. Instead, following the law was an expected response to God's deliverance. The

9. Rom 6:18.
10. Exod 3:8, 17.
11. Exod 3:7–8.
12. Exod 12:12.
13. Exod 12:13.
14. Exod 12:5.
15. Exod 20.

Hebrew people were called to live under a new code, a new law, because they were removed from the oppression of a tyrant, from a civilization opposed to God, from a culture removed from God, from a power keeping them in bondage and suffering, and instead brought into the kingdom of God.

The amazing lesson from Exodus is also to never go back into slavery. While this may sound basic, on multiple occasions the Hebrew people made efforts and expressed desire to leave the wilderness, abandon their dependence upon God, and instead return to the oppression of Egypt where they were comfortable.[16] Do not go back. Having been set free from sin, having been made into a new creation,[17] do not return to the bondage of slavery. Paul writes, "Put off your old self, which belongs to your former manner of life and is corrupt through deceitful desires."[18] But again, this new self was made available by the blood of the lamb, and not your own efforts.

Salvation Is Not from Your Efforts

In the Sermon on the Mount, Jesus teaches that not all who call him Lord will enter heaven.[19] This passage has often been discussed from a position of fear; no one wants to discover that they did not know him despite all their efforts to serve him. But this passage should be read with hope and comfort. The people in the passage boast about the actions done in the name of Jesus (prophesying, casting out demons, many mighty works)[20] as if these actions have earned them entrance into the kingdom of heaven. In reality, nothing that we do—sit with that statement: nothing that we do—determines our salvation. There is no act of faithfulness pure enough to bestow upon us a heavenly reward; likewise, there

16. Exod 16:3, 17:3.
17. 2 Cor 5:17.
18. Eph 4:22.
19. Matt 7:21.
20. Matt 7:22.

is no conduct so vile as to negate our opportunity to call upon the love of Christ. Shakespeare wrote, "In the course of Justice, none of us should see salvation: we do pray for mercie, and that same prayer doth teach us all to render the deeds of mercie."[21] There may also be a reason why C. S. Lewis depicted one of his most famous characters as growing in the understanding of both grace and justice; Edmund Pevensie was the traitor doomed to die and his redemption would cost the highest price. The Great Lion, the one who sang creation into being, would take his place upon the sacrificial altar; this is not an impersonal atonement for the masses, but a direct and intimate propitiation. In the end, Edmund would be crowned and be known for all his days as a graver and quieter man, great in council—King Edmund the Just.[22] When we understand the depth of the love displayed, mercy begets mercy. Other stories, of course, tell other tales.

According to Egyptian mythology, the last barrier to the entrance into eternal life was the judgment scales; the Egyptians taught that in the end your heart would be weighed against a feather—if you in life held onto the weariness of the world and did not combat worldly struggles with remarkably good deeds, eternal life would be denied.[23] Not only does basic science teach that a heart will indeed always weigh more than a feather, it may also be safe to say none of us would choose to have our lives weighed against such impossible standards. Thankfully, this is not the message and hope of the gospel. Because of the blessed mercy of Christ Jesus, there is no righteous deed or wretched sin so great as to determine our eternity. If it were any other way, we would stand doomed and without hope.

> Whoever believes in him is not condemned, but whoever does not believe is condemned already, because he has not believed in the name of the only Son of God.[24]

21. Shakespeare, *Merchant of Venice*, 350.
22. See Lewis, *Complete Chronicles of Narnia*, 132.
23. Taylor, *Journey Through the Afterlife*, 212.
24. John 3:18.

And yet it appears built into the nature of man that we should choose to be judged (and judge ourselves) purely by the sweat of our brow. Even the Israelites, time and time again, returned to teaching that salvation was only offered and maintained through adherence to the law rather than through faith. The apostles, in their various letters, challenged this false theology that became normative throughout the church; the call, instead, was to return to the original message of the gospel and not stray from the grace of Christ.[25] Still today the gates of heaven have been described as a place where we will have to explain or list the deeds of our life. But the conversation in heaven may be different than our legalistic expectations. Contrary to what most believe, we do not make ourselves clean for the purpose of being presentable and lovable to God. Instead, we remember that "God is love."[26] Augustine once said, "You called me; you cried aloud to me; you broke my barrier of deafness. You shone upon me; your radiance enveloped me; you put my blindness to flight. You shed your fragrance about me."[27] I was one thing, but now I am something different. To say I have been saved may not be enough; I am new. This is not of me; I cannot recreate myself.[28] Sit with the beauty and grace of what Jesus taught: nothing that *we* do determines our salvation.

Some may say, "LORD, I tried so hard to be a good person, a person of good Christian character. I strived to be generous. I attended church regularly. I even preached about your goodness." Christ will reply, "But did you know me?"

Others may in shame and regret mutter under heavy breath, "LORD, look away from me; I am a wretched sinner. I couldn't get anything right in my life. I am a complete failure and an embarrassment. I don't deserve anything." And Christ will reply, "But did you know me?"

In a sermon, Brennan Manning once shared that he had become convinced that the only question we will be asked at the

25. Gal 1:6–24.

26. 1 John 4:8.

27. Augustine, *Confessions*, 232.

28. See 2 Cor 5:17.

gates of heaven will be, "Did you believe that I loved you?"[29] To know the love of God, to know that Christ died for you, to put your faith and trust in the grace of God, to fall into the arms of Jesus and rest in his love, to rely on him as your hope and salvation, is to know Jesus.

29. Woodcrest Chapel, "Brennan Manning," 0:28.

Questions to Ponder

1. How often do you find yourself trying to earn your salvation? How can you break this habit?
2. What about the heart of Jesus from the Gospel of John stands out to you the most?
3. Have you ever thought about Exodus as being the salvation story? Does reading Exodus this way change the way you read and/or respond to the Gospels?
4. While this may sound overly simple, it deserves pause and meditation: Do you know Jesus?

Prayer

Father,

"In loving me, you made me lovable."

Amen.

CHAPTER 4

Divine Romance

Recommended Reading: Song of Songs, Job, Hosea, Revelation

In an interview, the famous psychiatrist Carl Jung was once asked if he believed in God; he responded, instead, that he *knew* God.[1] This is an important distinction. Can we say to ourselves that we do not simply believe in God but rather know him deeply, intimately, and personally. This is the relationship to which we are invited. Reading through Hosea, we discover that the prophet is giving us the intimate heart of God; after describing our shameful and adulterous nature, our continued unfaithfulness in our relationship with God, the LORD shares the remarkable depth of his love—he will do more than simply remain faithful while we are unfaithful. Hosea is ordered by God to marry an adulterous woman who will remain unrepentant—she will continue to have multiple affairs throughout their marriage. And this is representative of our relationship with God. Thankfully, instead of responding as expected, God responds with unfathomable mercy. When discussing the prophets, scholars

1. Freeman, "Face to Face," 7:49.

often describe God as the wounded lover.[2] His heart is broken over the state of his relationship with his bride, but he's not done. Read through Hosea and *know* his heart.

> She burned offerings to them and adorned herself with her ring and jewelry, and went after her lovers and forgot me, declares the LORD. Therefore, behold, I will allure her, and bring her into the wilderness, and speak tenderly to her.[3]

In response to our adultery, God seeks to seduce us back into an intimate relationship in which we were alone, dependent, and intimate with him in the wilderness. This may be the most beautiful "therefore" in all of recorded history. Read it again, but this time emphasize the "therefore, behold" and whisper the "I will allure her." Did you know that God is constantly alluring you, seducing you, beckoning you to return to intimacy? At the time of Hosea, God's people have turned to worshiping Baal: a god of plenty, a god of harvest, a god of prosperity. But God is making a statement: the God of heaven brings us to a bountiful harvest even in desolate lands; in places where nothing grows our God brings manna from heaven,[4] water from stones,[5] and honey from rocks.[6] This is the one who beckons us, allures us, seduces us back into intimacy with him.

Is this the God that you know? Is this the God that you encounter in prayer? Is this the LORD that you worship? Please let yourself read, meditate, and pray through Song of Songs.

The Bridegroom

The most beautiful depiction of the divine romance is sung through the Song of Songs; often misunderstood as fanciful love

2. Yancey, "God, the Jilted Lover," 72.
3. Hos 2:13–14.
4. Exod 16.
5. Exod 17.
6. Deut 32:13; Ps 81:16.

poetry equivalent to Shakespearean sonnets, the poetic, biblical song following the courtship and marriage of two lovers is instead categorized by scholars as wisdom literature—not history, law, or poetry. Wisdom. The poetic song is thought to best be categorized with the greatest teachings of the Bible. Then, while seemingly unconventional, the pairing of Song of Songs with Proverbs, Job, and Ecclesiastes allows us an adventure into the heart of God, to follow the course of a teaching. For instance, through Proverbs, we learn the perfect nature of all things (the promises of wisdom and the fate of folly); the story of Job, a legal playwright, however, challenges our demands and entitlements (that there should always be blessings for the righteous), instead pointing us to the message of Ecclesiastes. Now, from a purely expository approach, the message of Ecclesiastes can be seen as depressing: "Vanity of vanities, says the Preacher, vanity of vanities! All is vanity."[7] The conclusion of Ecclesiastes, after making it clear that everything is a "chasing after the wind,"[8] is that there is something to which we can hold: all that matters is God.

There is, however, wisdom and comfort to be found. We are not left to sit in the void of vanity alone: there is one that does not fade. If Ecclesiastes forces us without remorse to face and mourn harsh realities, Song of Songs seduces us. The song's poetry bewitches us into the only reality with meaning: God himself.

> My beloved speaks and says to me:
> "Arise, my love, my beautiful one, and come away,
> for behold, the winter is past; the rain is over and gone.
> The flowers appear on the earth,
> the time for singing has come,
> and the voice of the turtledove is heard in our land.
> The fig tree ripens its figs,
> and the vines are in blossom;
> they give forth fragrance.

7. Eccl 1:2.
8. Eccl 1:14.

> Arise, my love, my beautiful one,
> and come away."[9]

We are allured, seduced, beckoned to "come away" and be able to proclaim with loving assurance that "my beloved is mine, and I am his."[10] Even within the book of Proverbs, we must begin to recognize the relational language; it is not a collection of fortune cookie statements demanding obedience. We are implored to pursue Lady Wisdom, to dine with her, to hear her voice.[11] Adding to this sentiment, we find that Proverbs is best read and understood as a dialogue; it is not a collection of proverbs, but a dialogue of guidance, of wisdom, of mentorship, between father and son[12] ending with wisdom best being personified by the child's mother—her worth far more valuable than rubies.[13] Lady Wisdom beckons us to follow a harder path and, in the end, join the banqueting table within the room laden with the fullness of life.[14]

God Loves His Bride

Passages from Song of Songs are rarely read from the pulpit; this may be partly due to the specific nature of the descriptions used. "The daring metaphor of Jesus as bridegroom suggests that the living God seeks more than an intimate relationship with us."[15] The bridegroom describes his love for his bride, he describes everything physically glorious about her, and he doesn't miss a section of her body; the message is clear: "You are altogether beautiful, my love."[16]

9. Song 2:10–13.
10. Song 2:16.
11. Prov 9:5–6.
12. Prov 1:8.
13. Prov 31:10–31.
14. Prov 9:1–3.
15. Manning, *Furious Longing of God*, 30.
16. Song 4:7.

We have all heard that God knows us and loves us. But take the time now to sit with that truth. God sees you. He knows you. He loves you. He likes you. Unfortunately, "Christians find it easier to believe that God exists than that God loves them."[17] But we serve a God who does not look away; he is captivated by the beauty of his bride. He walks beside her and uplifts her; he adorns her with fine linens and silks;[18] he covers her with jewelry and places a crown on her head.[19] He does not brood over his creation as a tyrant judge of wrath—God gazes upon his bride as a lover: "You grew exceedingly beautiful and advanced to royalty."[20] The God of heaven is a romantic whose heart is set on you! Again, is *this* the God you know? Kierkegaard writes, "To cheat oneself out of love is the most terrible deception; it is an eternal loss for which there is no reparation."[21] Don't shy away from the lavish romanticism of the love of God; read Scripture and let it make you blush!

A similar picture of the extravagant love of God is also painted through the prophet Isaiah. His people, scattered throughout the world in exile, are reminded of the basic truth of God's faithfulness. He is with them. This is even despite the fact that they are living in exile due to their unfaithfulness; but God is not bitter or resentful, and he does not gloat in their punishment. On the contrary, he presses into faithfulness towards them: "But now thus says the Lord, he who created you, O Jacob, he who formed you, O Israel: 'Fear not for I have redeemed you; I have called you by name, you are mine.'"[22] The echoes of Song of Songs are clear: "I am my beloved's and his desire is for me"[23]—our God does not change. "You are mine."[24] As he continues, he comforts his people

17. Manning, *Furious Longing of God*, 76.

18. Ezek 16:10.

19. Ezek 16:11–12.

20. Ezek 16:13.

21. Kierkegaard, *Works of Love*, 23.

22. Isa 43:1.

23. Song 7:10.

24. Isa 43:1.

with the reminder that no matter the circumstances he will personally walk with them.

> When you pass through waters, I will be with you; and through the rivers, they shall not overwhelm you. When you walk through fire, you shall not be burned; and the flame shall not consume you. For I am the LORD your God, the Holy One of Israel, your Savior. I give Egypt as your ransom, Cush and Seba in exchange for you. Because you are precious in my eyes, and honored, and I love you, I give men in return for you, peoples in exchange for your life. Fear not, for I am with you.[25]

Precious. Honored. Loved. He continues to clarify his position toward you by adding defining statements of your place in his heart. The one who formed you, the one who created the heavens and earth, the Holy One, holds you in a place of honor because you are the precious bride of a jealous[26] lover who watches your steps, guards your path, and holds you as beautifully fit for heavenly royalty.[27] Is *this* the God you know?

The God Who Suffers

We serve a God willing to suffer, to join us in our suffering, in pursuit of reunion with us. Through the prophet Isaiah, we are given the prophecy of Christ where he is the suffering servant who took on our grief, sorrow, afflictions, and transgressions that we might have peace.[28] While working through his grief after the death of his son, Wolterstorff comes to a remarkable conclusion:

> God is love. That is why he suffers. To love our suffering sinful world is to suffer. God so suffered for the world that he gave up his only Son to suffering. The one who does not see God's suffering does not see his love. God is

25. Isa 43:2–5.
26. Exod 20:5.
27. Ezek 16:13.
28. Isa 52:13—53:12.

> suffering love. So suffering is down at the center of things, deep down where the meaning is. Suffering is the meaning of our world. For Love is the meaning. And Love suffers. The tears of God are the meaning of history.[29]

We do not serve a cold and distant divine being who is all-powerful but emotionless and unmoved. Our God moves. Our God pursues us with passion, longing, and even heartache. He suffers because of his love for us.

Unchallenged and Holy

We must also understand that our divine romance is not with an emotional sentimentalist. We are pursued and allured by the unchallenged, unrivaled, holy authority of heaven. As we read through Job and Revelation, we see one undebatable truth: God is in charge.

The book of Job begins with God interacting with Satan. The enemy wanders through heaven and God starts a calm conversation.[30] He is not challenged or frightened. The kingdom of heaven was not in jeopardy because of the presence of Satan. Likewise, in Revelation we are told that in the end Christ will return in power and glory and vanquish his enemies—the great war between heaven and hell does not last very long.[31] The same story can be seen in the Gospels; when Jesus encounters those possessed by demons, the demonic forces shudder—they even beg him for mercy.[32] God wins. We need not fear the demonic forces; our God is greater. Our attention should not be on the fear that the enemy attempts to conjure—it should be on Christ.

Many describe a fanciful struggle between heaven and hell as though God *can* be challenged. But this is not the truth of the Bible. The story of Job ends with God finally answering Job's legal

29. Wolterstorff, *Lament for a Son*, 90.
30. Job 1:6–12.
31. Rev 19:11–21.
32. Mark 5:1–20.

complaints. Through the story, Job challenged God by objectifying him; he first assumes that he knows best and then wrongly presumes that he can hold God accountable for not fulfilling the role that he dictated (God should bless the righteous and curse the wicked). God's answer is simple: I, the Lord, am in charge, not you.[33]

Likewise, when Moses was brought before the burning bush, he was given a mission that appeared to be beyond his capabilities. As someone raised and educated in a royal Egyptian household, he was familiar with the gods of Egypt; these gods have assigned roles and can be held accountable to the ideals to which they have been assigned. A safe assumption, then, is that his question is less practical than it is personal: Moses asked, "Who shall I say sent me?"[34] This very well may be a question seeking definitive clarity on the assigned roles and duties of God. Instead, the Lord replies, "I will be what I will be."[35] The response is simple: "I, the Lord, am above all—you cannot hold me accountable. I am the standard."

33. Job 38–41.

34. Exod 3:13.

35. Exod 3:14.

Questions to Ponder

1. What misconceptions about God have you had? Are you still holding on to any?
2. Do you know that God loves you?
3. Do you know that God likes you?

Prayer

Lord God, my love,

You are beautiful, my beloved, truly delightful.[36] *Draw me after you; let us run.*[37] *I am yours, and you are mine.*[38]

Amen.

36. Song 1:16.
37. Song 1:4.
38. Song 6:3.

CHAPTER 5

Turning to God

Recommended Reading: Amos

Throughout the Bible, the message of our need for repentance is consistent and essential. However, despite the consistent messaging, the heart of repentance is widely misunderstood. As a start, we need to accept that our need for repentance is nonnegotiable. It was the message of the prophets in the Old Testament. It was the message of John the Baptist as he prepared the hearts of God's people for the coming messiah.[1] And it was the message that Christ preached when he first started his ministry.[2] "Repent for the kingdom of heaven is at hand" is a very clear message. Therefore, repentance is essential. Next, we need to understand that our repentance does not result in our salvation; the apostle Paul is very clear on the source of our salvation:

> For by grace you have been saved through faith, and this is not of your own doing; it is the gift of God, not the result of works, so that no one may boast.[3]

1. Matt 3:1–3.
2. Matt 4:17.
3. Eph 2:8–9.

We are saved only by the grace of God, by the work of Christ on the cross (not our works and efforts—which includes our efforts to repent), by nothing but the blood of Jesus. But again, repentance is essential; if we accept Jesus as our savior but refuse to follow him and leave our sinful ways, we refuse to surrender to his lordship. It should be clearly understood that an unrepentant heart rejects Jesus and thereby also rejects his salvation. One example we are given of this truth is the story of the man who was forgiven much but refused to forgive others.[4] He was forgiven of a significant debt but then refused to follow in the likeness of his master; the result was his return to condemnation. The issue with the man from this parable is the state of his heart; because he did not understand the salvation he was offered and because he refused to follow his master's ways, his heart was not positioned for repentance. As a parent, I am reminded of this story often.

I have two amazing children; but of course there are some teaching opportunities that arise from time to time. For instance, my children start their day—every day—with household chores; the tasks are simple and suited to each accordingly. When I have them race or try to beat a timer, the chores are done in no time at all. I also occasionally help them with their chores; while I do enjoy finding something tangible to do with my hands, and I do enjoy working, I also sometimes just want to make my children's lives easier. After all, we all need a blessing and a hand up from time to time. However, despite the generosity of the blessing, I have found that it is not always paid forward. The one that I helped enjoys the break, runs to lounge on the couch, and then stubbornly refuses to help either their mother or sibling with a very simple task. I wish I could say that this scenario was rare. I also wish I could say that I was never guilty of it myself. Again, this is an issue of a heart posture that is unrepentant (refusing to turn and follow) because the gift that was offered is being taken for granted.

Consider another simple example. If my children confessed with their lips that my wife and I were in charge, that we were the adults who make the rules, that we were the king and queen of the

4. Matt 18:21–35.

family, then completely refused to listen to or obey a single word we said, would their statement of belief have any meaning at all? Likewise, if I say that Christ is King, but then crown myself with all authority, of what value are my declarations about Christ? Repentance (turning and following) is the action backing my statements of belief. Christ is my Lord and Savior; therefore, I will turn from my own ways and instead follow him.

It is also important to understand that there are two simultaneous conversations occurring; and, because of that, we need to be clear of our definitions and meanings. First, we must understand the simplicity of repentance: turning to God. In this understanding, salvation is made available to us, the longing of God to lavish mercy upon us is released simply because we turn to him. This is not a journey of great length (although it is the most important journey of your life), and it doesn't matter how far away you've run—the moment you turn, he is there. More accurately, he was always there just waiting for you to turn your eyes to him: "Come to me, all who labor and are heavy laden, and I will give you rest."[5] He wants us, has pleaded with us, to turn to him to be saved:

> If my people who are called by my name humble themselves, and pray and seek my face and turn from their wicked ways, then I will hear from heaven and will forgive their sin and heal their land.[6]

> Repent therefore, and turn back, that your sins may be blotted out.[7]

> "For I have no pleasure in the death of anyone," declares the Lord God; "so turn, and live."[8]

> For thus says the Lord to the house of Israel: "Seek me and live."[9]

5. Matt 11:28.
6. 2 Chr 7:14.
7. Acts 3:19.
8. Ezek 18:32.
9. Amos 5:4.

Scripture clearly outlines the truth that we desperately need to turn to him, and, when we do, *he* saves us out of his abundant mercy. And it must be said and emphasized that all who call upon the name of Jesus will be saved.[10] If you have never done so, now is the time! However, to end the conversation here would be a mistake; because, now having turned to him (having repented) and having received his merciful salvation, we are now called to live in repentance. Remember the story of the man who was forgiven much; he turned to his master and pleaded for his master's mercy (repentance) and abundant mercy was bestowed (salvation); now, forgiven of much, he was expected to move forward by living in repentance (following the ways of his master). It is often confused that following him, living according to his ways, will result in your salvation; instead, it must be understood that living in repentance in order to obtain salvation is futile legalism. Our faith, in direct opposition to all other religious teachings, teaches that blessing precedes requirement. Works-based religions teach that requirement will result in blessing; but the gospel boldly proclaims the hope that blessing comes free and paves the way for living in accordance with the kingdom of God. We must live *in* repentance. But this is because it is a response to the abundant mercy of Christ. Turn to God and be saved; then live in repentance, live in a new way.

In the story of the adulterous woman,[11] we can also see these truths depicted with an emphasis placed on the order of events. In this story, a woman caught in adultery is brought before Jesus by the Pharisees and made to stand before the crowd ashamed. While it may be curious as to why the woman's partner was not also brought out in condemnation or why this woman was publicly shamed before her inevitable execution, it may be a glimpse into the condition of the sickened hearts of those present who are so eager to stand in a place of judgment. Perhaps to our surprise today, we read in the story that Jesus does not argue against the judgment. He did not make a stand as the woman's defense

10. Rom 10:13.

11. John 8:1–11.

counsel. Jesus never said that the conclusion of the mob was incorrect or inappropriate; for, indeed, the wages of sin is death.[12] Instead, he writes in the sand and presents one condition for the execution: "Let anyone among you who is without sin be the first to throw a stone at her."[13] While Jesus continues to write in the sand, the crowd disperses, dropping their stones as they leave. Scripture does not specify what was written, so nothing definitive can be said about it. However, it has long been assumed that Jesus was writing the sins of those holding stones. We should pause here for a moment and take note that there is something beautiful about having your sins written in sand instead of chiseled in stone. As the story continues, the only one capable of condemning the woman then turned to her stating, "Neither do I condemn you."[14] She stood condemned—a sinner deserving death—before a holy judge who instead gave grace and salvation; all that was written in the sand was wiped clean as if it had never been there. However, this is not the end of the story. Jesus continued, "Go, and from now on sin no more."[15] Pay attention to the order: condemnation, grace, living in repentance.

Our Response to Grace

Again, living in repentance does not bring our salvation. Instead, it is a response to the grace of Jesus. Grace was offered to us, Christ died in our place for our salvation while we were still unrepentant.[16] Then, having been saved, repent. We often think, "I'll repent, then God . . ." However, this is a backwards understanding. Repentance is a response to God's salvation. But what does it mean to repent? If we desire to live repentant lives that honor God, we

12. Rom 6:23.
13. John 8:7.
14. John 8:11; see John 3:17.
15. John 8:11.
16. Rom 5:8.

have to know what it means to be truly repentant. And there are a lot of things which repentance is not.

Repentance is not merely being sorrowful for our sin. The self-condemnation and act of self-flogging can quickly become a practice of self-idolatry in which we assume the role of godly judge over our own souls. To be penitent can be good, but the habit of forcing ourselves to make penance to God is an insult to the grace of the cross and ignores the heart of biblical repentance.

Repentance is also not making a promise to God to never sin again. As a start, he knows this is a promise that you cannot keep. Also, repentance and righteousness should not be understood as the avoidance of breaking the law or as a line in the sand to avoid crossing. Repentance, rather, is a direction. Consider:

> When you are unsatisfied with the Christian life, when you are overcome with dryness and boredom, the only question that really matters is: Lord, where are you in the midst of this? If you focus on the reason this is happening, you will become lost. Maybe it is because of your sin, but what can you do about that other than turn to the Lord? We misinterpret what the Lord is calling us to because many of us turn to self-help in the exact place the Lord is calling us to abide. In the midst of our sin we starting thinking, *I'll do better next time, God*. Or, *I'll fix this soon, I promise*. Or even, *Let me prove to you I'm worthy of your sacrifice*. All these are nothing less than idolatry and self-help. They are idolatry because they are oriented to a god other than the Christian God. They are self-help because they assume that God wants us to get our lives in order before he will be with us. These lies forget that it was while we were in our sin that he died for us, and that without him, we can do nothing.[17]

Turn to God

The word repentance means turning. To repent is to turn or change directions. Again, repentance is a direction. It is not a practice of

17. Goggin and Strobel, *Beloved Dust*, 20–21. Emphasis original.

adhering to a list of dos and don'ts; it's about chasing after God, seeking him; it's about following Jesus.

Amos was a prophet at a very strange time is Israel's history. As you read through the book of Amos, pay particular notice to the dichotomy. The prophet Jeremiah wails loudly at the destruction of Jerusalem because of the abhorrent decisions of the king. Jonah doesn't even speak to God's people; Jonah is sent as an evangelist to the enemies of God's people. Elijah is a prophet at a time in which God's people are serving other gods. But Amos is speaking at a time when God's people are faithful in ritualistic religious practices, a time of prosperity, a time of comfort. It is during this time of comfort that Amos prophesies of Israel's destruction, and, through that prophecy, we are given a picture of the heart of God and a description of true repentance.

Through Amos, we read of the dichotomy between loveless religious practices and the heart of God. God describes their engagement in loveless spiritual disciplines as repulsive and unacceptable to him. They are worshiping. They are praising. They are sacrificing. But something very important is missing.

> I hate, I despise your feasts, and I take no delight in your solemn assemblies. Even though you offer me your burnt offerings and grain offerings, I will not accept them; and the peace offerings of your fattened animals, I will not look upon them. Take away from me the noise of your songs; to the melody of your harps I will not listen.[18]

We read earlier in Amos that, despite the regular presence of religious and biblical activities and adherence to the law, their hearts were far from God. Daily spiritual practices did not result in God-honoring behaviors and attitudes.

> They sell the righteous for silver, and the needy for a pair of sandals—those who trample the head of the poor into the dust of the earth.[19]

18. Amos 5:21–23.

19. Amos 2:6–7.

The response from God is loving and compassionate; he pours out his heart and calls his people to repentance:

> Seek me and live.[20]
>
> Seek the LORD and live.[21]
>
> Seek good, and not evil, that you may live.[22]

At the heart of living in repentance is seeking the LORD. When we are chasing after him, moving his direction, we are actively turning from our own paths, refusing to following our former direction, and, instead, pursuing the ways of God. It is also important to note that God's call for our repentance is for our own good; he wants us to avoid the coming danger and destruction and instead find life.[23] Instead of the loveless religious rituals, God, through Amos, required them to pursue righteousness, to make the pursuit of right-standing with God a constant effort. And this includes imitating the Father's heart. These are the actions of a repentant heart:

> But let justice roll down like waters, and righteousness like an ever-flowing stream.[24]

20. Amos 5:4.
21. Amos 5:6.
22. Amos 5:14.
23. John 10:10.
24. Amos 5:24.

Questions to Ponder

1. What does turning toward God and wholeheartedly pursuing him look like in your life?
2. How can you know if you are simply following a routine and engaging in religious practices without a proper heart posture instead of living a life in pursuit of righteousness? What evidence would you consider?
3. Do you ever find yourself being penitent in the hope that God will forgive you?
4. What can you do to step into the grace and salvation that Christ has already offered you?

Prayer

Lord,

I praise you and thank you for your steadfast mercy and grace. You are good, Lord, and you are good to me. Help me, Father, to remain repentant, to chase fervently after you with all of my heart, mind, and strength. I want to be a person after your own heart.

Amen.

CHAPTER 6

A New Way to Live

Recommended Reading: 1 and 2 Peter, James

One of the oldest debates in the church has been on the topic of grace and works. On one side of the spectrum is the argument that works are not expected and not possible until Christ returns and there is a new heaven and new earth. Church leaders like Luther and Calvin argued that even the Sermon on the Mount points to a way of living that is not possible and therefore the entire sermon points to nothing but grace. Meanwhile, on the other side of the debate, the church has always included a large group of believers who still promote a legalistic perspective in which grace is earned and proven through deeds.

This should not be a dividing issue in the church; instead, we only need to turn to Scripture. Paul clearly states, "For it is by grace you have been saved, through faith. And this is not from your own doing; it is the gift of God, not a result of works, so that no one may boast."[1] We are not saved by our good deeds. But this does not eliminate our need for good deeds—works still have a place. As you read through James, pay attention to his discussion of deeds.

1. Eph 2:8–9.

> Someone will say, "You have faith and I have works." Show me your faith apart from your works, and I will show you my faith by my works.[2]

The two are joined together. They must be together; it is not possible to have a beautiful faith without the outward display of good works. "For sweetest things turn sowrest by their deedes. Lillies that fester smell far worse than weeds."[3] James continues, "For as the body apart from the spirit is dead, so also faith apart from works is dead."[4] The debate on grace and works is not a conversation of *or* but rather *and*. We need to know the relationship between the two and keep ourselves biblically founded. The problem of leaning away from the conversation about works is that we abandon the commandments of God and instead live a worldly life. But if we forgo the gift of amazing grace and focus our efforts on works we become legalistic Pharisees burdened by the law; we also insult the sacrifice of Christ by assuming that we are capable of saving ourselves without his sacrifice.

A New Way to Live

We are called to follow Jesus,[5] to live as he lived. He is our example, and we are to imitate him and be led by the Spirit through those efforts. We have been saved by the blood of the Lamb; we have been redeemed by Christ; we have been called his; and to show our love and gratitude, we follow him.[6] Just as the Hebrews were given a new way of life (the Law) *after* being delivered from the afflictions of Egypt, so we too are shown a new path after being mercifully saved by graced. Again, James writes that faith is active and made complete with works.[7] How can we say we love Jesus

2. Jas 2:18.
3. Shakespeare, *Sonnet 94*, 84.
4. Jas 2:26.
5. Matt 4:19; Mark 1:17.
6. John 14:15.
7. Jas 2:22.

while ignoring everything he has to say about how to live our lives? Our devotion, then, is a response to grace. We leave behind our sinful ways and choose to walk in the light.[8] As you read through 1 and 2 Peter, write down two things:

1. What are we to put away?
2. What are we to make every effort to pursue?

Make Every Effort

Peter is very specific in outlining this new way of living. We are to put away our old ways, our ways before encountering Christ; and we are to take up and make every effort towards[9] following a new way of living. Scholar and author Walter Brueggemann said it like this: "Live in fervent anticipation of the newness that God has promised and will surely give."[10] And again, Peter begins his list with the statement, "Since you have been born again,"[11] followed by, "Put away all malice and all deceit and hypocrisy and envy and all slander."[12] Malice. Deceit. Hypocrisy. Envy. Slander. We are to rid ourselves of these behaviors, to put them far behind us. These five things have no place in the church or the Christian life. While this may appear to be a short list, each are individually capable of destroying lives and dividing the church—and they are easy behaviors to fall into if we are not careful. The apostle Paul gives a similar description in Ephesians; he calls us to put off walking as gentiles do: hardness of heart, callousness, sensuality, greedy to practice every kind of impurity, corruption, falsehood, theft, corrupt talking, bitterness, wrath, anger, clamor, slander, malice, and deceitful desires.[13] The Bible is clear on what we are to stop doing now that we belong to Christ.

8. 1 John 1:7.
9. 2 Pet 1:5–15.
10. Brueggemann, *Prophetic Imagination*, 3.
11. 1 Pet 1:23.
12. 1 Pet 2:1.
13. Eph 4:17–31.

Furthermore, now that we have put away our former selves,[14] we are not to be left empty-handed; as we read in 1 and 2 Peter, we are to take up: preparing our minds for action, being sober-minded, hoping fully on grace,[15] honoring everyone, loving the brotherhood, fearing God,[16] living as servants,[17] being understanding with our spouses,[18] having unity of mind, being sympathetic, showing brotherly love, being tender hearted, having a humble mind, blessing others, keeping our tongues from evil and our lips from speaking deceit, turning away from evil, doing good, seeking peace and pursuing it,[19] being gentle, showing respect,[20] being self-controlled, keeping on loving, showing hospitality (*without grumbling*), serving one another,[21] shepherding the flock of God, being Christ-like examples to each other,[22] supplementing our faith with virtue and knowledge and self-control, remaining steadfast in godliness, showing brotherly affection and love, and being diligent to the calling of Christ.[23] Needless to say, we have a lot of work to do! But it is also clear that the message is consistent throughout the Bible. Moses presents before the people of God the basic choice that they all must make: "I have set before you life and death, blessing and curse. Therefore choose life, that you and your offspring may live."[24] Likewise, the book of Proverbs calls us to choose Lady Wisdom and not follow the snares of Madam Folly. Peter continued these teachings by instructing us to put off what we were and instead clothe ourselves in the ways of God.

14. Eph 4:22.
15. 1 Pet 1:13.
16. 1 Pet 2:15.
17. 1 Pet 2:16.
18. 1 Pet 3:7.
19. 1 Pet 3:8–11.
20. 1 Pet 3:15.
21. 1 Pet 4:7–10.
22. 1 Pet 5:2–3.
23. 2 Pet 1:5–10.
24. Exod 30:19.

We must also note that these actions cannot be achieved without a heart postured in humility toward obedience to Christ. It is not about simply *doing*. Making every effort to walk in godliness and righteousness is to work out our salvation[25] allowing for the heart of God to lead us in sanctification. This is a primary role of the Holy Spirit—to lead us in sanctification.[26] The Spirit speaks, guides, helps, convicts, encourages, teaches. However, through our efforts and our pleading with God, we must remember that making every effort is not about *doing*, it is about *becoming*. "One of the great tragedies of life is to become so busy *doing* that we stop *becoming*."[27] But we must be intentional as to *what* we are becoming.

Become Like Children

In his letter, Peter does not call us to a cheap and easy faith; we are challenged to take on a remarkable faith that not only asks much of us but requires that we devote *all* of ourselves. But we should not be discouraged. If you read the list above and find it to be daunting—you're probably not alone—take heart because we are not left alone on this difficult journey.

Jesus taught us that in order to enter the kingdom of heaven, we must become like children.[28] This, obviously, does not mean being childish and immature; instead, a child following a loving parent excitedly runs and jumps into the outstretched arms willingly surrendering themselves with amazing trust to the one who loves them so dearly. Speaking as the father, Manning writes,

> My child, fan the flame of your confidence in Me. Keep it burning. I want you to be happy, to come back again and again to this feeling of trust until you are never without it. Trust is an aspect of love. If you love Me

25. Phil 2:12.
26. Rom 15:16; 1 Pet 1:2.
27. Kopp, *Gospel for a New People*, 13.
28. Matt 18:3–4.

> and believe in My love for you, you will surrender your whole self into My hands like a little child who doesn't even ask, "Where are your taking me?" but sets off joyously, hand in hand.[29]

Beware of Idolatry

When focusing on living out the virtues of the Christian life, putting on the new self, and making every effort to conduct ourselves in a manner worthy of Christ, we still must remain watchful that we do not create for ourselves idols.[30] Idols are, in fact, anything that we worship instead of God. While we are commanded to follow Christ and live according to his ways, when we focus all of our efforts on our good works, there is a temptation to fall into the practice of idolatry of self—praising *our* good works instead of glorifying the Father in heaven. For any who believe, or have been taught, that the Christian life can measured by specific deeds, we must remember that the Father is far more concerned with the state of our hearts; again, Kierkegaard argues,

> There is no deed, not a single one, not even the best, of which we dare to say unconditionally: he who does this thereby unconditionally demonstrates love. It depends upon *how* the deed is done. There are, indeed, acts which in a special sense are called works of love. But, in truth, because one makes charitable contributions, because he visits the widow and clothes the naked—his love is not necessarily demonstrated or made recognisable by such deeds, for one can perform works of love in an unloving, yes even in a self-loving way.[31]

"The discipline, by the way," as Eldredge argued, "is never the point. The whole point of a 'devotional life' is *connecting with God*. This is our primary antidote to the counterfeits the world holds out to us. If you do not have God and have him deeply, you

29. Manning, *Relentless Tenderness of Jesus*, 76.

30. Exod 20:4; Lev 26:1.

31. Kierkegaard, *Works of Love*, 30. Emphasis original.

will turn to other lovers."[32] And it should be noted that "other lovers" most often takes a turn toward love of self.

If we believe that our actions will bring us closer to God, then we find ourselves engaging in idolatry. The spiritual disciplines, the practicing of our faith, our healthy religious habits, are good, but they do not bring us closer to God. When our lives do not include the pursuit of the Father through reading his word or seeking him in prayer, it must be said that we are not *far* from God. Buber writes, "It is not the relation that necessarily grows feeble, but the actuality of its immediacy."[33] We do not pray to bring God close; we pray because God is close. We do not read our Bibles to make God want to be around us; he is with us. Instead, we read our Bibles to learn how close he already is. We do not worship God to make him love us; we worship because he loves us. We do not attend church in order to appear presentable to God; we gather together because God has invited us—sinners and ragamuffins—into his presence and made us beautiful in his sight. Again, Buber argues, "He who knows God knows also very well remoteness from God, and the anguish of barrenness in the tormented heart; but he does not know the absence of God: it is we only who are not always there."[34] This is not a matter of trifling semantics. To get the order wrong is to fall into the snares of idolatry.

32. Eldredge, *Wild at Heart*, 172. Emphasis original.

33. Buber, *I and Thou*, 95–96.

34. Buber, *I and Thou*, 96.

Questions to Ponder

1. We are told to put off malice, deceit, hypocrisy, envy, and slander. Which is the hardest to cease?
2. Of the many behaviors that we are to fervently pursue, which do you best display? Which is the hardest?
3. How does knowing that your behaviors do not change your position with Christ (nearness or distance) impact your walk with God?

Prayer

God,

Lead me in your ways. I long to have a heart that chases after yours. Teach me your ways and let my life be but a reflection of you. Guide me. Disciple me. Thank you for calling me to a new way to live. Help me to put the old behind me. I love you, O LORD, *and I want to obey you and live according to your will.*

Amen.

CHAPTER 7

Intentional Relationship

Recommended Reading: Proverbs, 1 and 2 Timothy

Many read through Proverbs as though it was a collection of random wise sayings; this fortune cookie approach to Proverbs can provide us with wise sayings and good practices, but we'll miss the heart and power of Proverbs with this approach. As we read through Proverbs, try paying particular notice to the parts of speech and metaphors implemented; what we'll notice is that Proverbs is first and foremost a conversation: "Hear, my son, your father's instruction, and forsake not your mother's teachings."[1] We know from the opening verses that the purpose of Proverbs is to provide wisdom, instruction, understanding, and fear of the LORD;[2] but verse 8 informs us of the audience. Proverbs is a conversation between father and son. What if we then read Proverbs as an instruction manual for discipleship? In this, we are given a beautiful depiction of discipleship as an intentional relationship between intimates.

1. Prov 1:8.
2. Prov 1:1–7.

Father to Son

Discipleship does not occur between strangers; it is not achieved by forming a brief class with a well structured curriculum. Discipleship is not created when someone who thinks he knows something tries to become an instructor to someone whom he has assessed to not know enough. Discipleship is not a program. Instead, it is only successfully accomplished between two individuals deeply connected with vested interests and intimate love. To speak directly to fathers for a minute: this is your role—love your children, raise them in the knowledge and understanding of the Lord, and be invested in their lives. However, this should not, obviously, be limited to only biological fathers and sons. In Paul's letters to Timothy, he refers to Timothy as his child:

> This charge I entrust to you, Timothy, my child.[3]
>
> To Timothy, my beloved child.[4]

Paul is discipling Timothy and taking on a role of an adopted father committed to his son, loving his son, instructing his son, encouraging his son . . . Paul is following the example provided in Proverbs. When we attempt to engage in discipleship from any other approach (for example: expert to novice) we lose the power of the discipleship relationship. It occurs within a loving and intentional relationship between two people who love each other. For this conversation, the word *love* cannot be used enough.

As you are considering being discipled (and you should be at any age), find someone whose heart is pointed in the right direction, someone you could submit to and love, someone who you respect. This does not mean finding a perfect person—they don't exist. It means searching for someone who is chasing after God. A good measure is to find someone who represents well Micah 6:8: "Seek justice, love mercy, and walk humbly with your God." And again, when discipleship is properly understood as a loving relationship between two people who are chasing after God with

3. 1 Tim 1:18.
4. 2 Tim 1:2.

the wisdom to know that it is best to not run that race alone, why would we not want to seek being discipled? The problem is that most of us have been given a terrible depiction. Intentionally or otherwise, the picture we have been given is far more related to classroom instruction. This typically leads older and more knowledgable Christians (especially those who have been in the church for a significant amount of time) to come to the false conclusion that they have graduated from the role of being discipled. This demographic may then feel led to only take on the role of discipling others, but they also could be led astray by the lies of inadequacies, assuming that they have nothing (or not enough) to teach others. Pastors across the country for decades have struggled to encourage a culture of discipleship within their churches and are also at a loss as to why the struggle is so difficult. To put it plainly, the problem is that we do not accurately teach what discipleship is.

Discipleship is a relationship between two people doing life together, following Christ together. In Proverbs, the father passes on to the son what he has learned. In the Gospels, Christ tells the Twelve what he has seen the Father doing.[5] Therefore, yes, we should pass on to those we are discipling what we have seen, read, heard, learned, etc. But I can also tell you that what I have learned can be summed up into two main truths. The first thing that I know is in regard to my identity: I am poor in spirit; I am a beggar before the cross of mercy; I was a sinner redeemed by the blood of Christ; I am no greater (or worse) than anyone around me; I am loved by God; Christ calls me his own. Secondly, I know that we should not walk this road alone. This simple understanding makes my approach to discipleship easy: as one ragamuffin to another, let's stick together.

On the other hand, we also need to remember to take measures to ensure that we are taking the discipleship relationship seriously. As you are looking to disciple another, check your heart and intentions. Ask yourself:

5. John 5:19–20.

1. Are you prepared to invest in a loving relationship with someone whom you will look upon as your own child?
2. Are you looking to build yourself up by playing the role of an expert or are you humbly following God and hoping to invest in the life of someone also on that journey?
3. Are you willing to be discipled by another or are you struggling with your own pride?

This is a high standard and a lot to ask. But the discipleship relationship is sacred and necessary for the Christian life. It deserves an incredibly high standard. Let us not treat it as a temporary interaction that can be discarded on a whim.

Transparent and Forthcoming

Practically speaking, Proverbs also sheds light on how to start the discipleship relationship: be transparent. Without transparency a relationship is based on deceit and ulterior motives—the result is no relationship at all. Proverbs 1:1–7 is very clear and concise in the purpose of the interaction; we should be too! Why are we gathering? What is the purpose of the discussions? While this transparency improves understanding and reduces the potential for confusion as to the intentions of the relationship, it also allows for both parties to enter into the meetings with mutual agreement. Overly clever minds attempt to manipulate situations and conversations to simulate the appearance of a naturally occurring discipleship relationship; the result, however, is quite the opposite. Instead, be forthcoming and honest.

Discipleship Is About Life

Within that transparent and intentional relationship, the father in Proverbs speaks to his son about all aspects of life; this is also reflected in Paul's relationship with Timothy. Paul gives specific pastoral instructions to Timothy, but he also encourages him personally and even addresses Timothy's health concerns. While there are some who discuss differences between various forms and intentions of mentorship, Proverbs shows us a different path. All of life is a spiritual matter.

Throughout Proverbs the father instructs his son on topics such as (but not limited to) the temptations of the world, how to live as a good citizen and neighbor, how to pursue a righteous life, how to interact with the poor, and how to conduct business. Wisdom and righteousness are not limited to discussions on prayer, worship, spiritual gifting, or Bible study. All matters are on the table because all matters are important to God. If we are pursuing wisdom in our life while entertaining foolishness in our business life, we stand both confused and deceived—everything becomes foolishness. As you are being discipled, open yourself to someone who will speak into your entire life. As you are discipling another, do not let yourself turn a blind eye to foolishness because that area of life was not on the meeting's agenda.

Discipleship Occurs Within Life

The conversation about understanding and applying wisdom to all aspects of life is a big topic that can understandably be overwhelming. Again, we turn to Proverbs. This huge topic is discussed through practical examples that the son can understand. The father speaks to his son primarily about women (as fathers should), and there are two women that his son can pursue: Lady Wisdom or Madam Folly. The father uses everyday examples to illustrate the struggles and temptations his son will face. He also gives his son an example that is observed every day: his mother. The often discussed Proverbs 31 is not a message particularly directed to women; instead, it is a continuation of the metaphor of wisdom seen throughout the conversation in Proverbs. While it obviously applies to women, and women are to heed it, it is clearly not limited to women. In fact, there should be (in addition to the countless number of books written for women on this topic) devotionals written for men based purely on Proverbs 31.

In this chapter, the father instructs his son to look to his mother's example of discipline, sacrifice, hard work, generosity, and industriousness. The message should be clear: wisdom is more than an intellectual discussion—it's a daily practice.

Discipleship, moreover, should not be constrained to an intellectual or philosophical discussion; it should exist within an intentional relationship between two people who are doing life together and using the examples of everyday life to further the understanding of wisdom. The one discipling can give real life examples because he knows deeply the one he is discipling; he is doing life with the one he is discipling; he has a relationship with the one he is discipling.

Healing Is Found in Relationship

I understand that, for some, the emphasis on relationships (over teaching and structure) sounds flowery and soft. Many of us hear the word *relationship* and immediately assume that the content is not robust. But this could not be further from the truth. Within psychology, it is well understood, and has been since the field's inception, that, while techniques and interventions may have some basic impact, healing only occurs within heartfelt relationships. In fact, without the relationship, no clinical progress can be made. Unfortunately, the psychological industry today has almost entirely abandoned this precept—primarily because the secular world fails to understand the meaning of genuine relationship. We, therapist and patient alike, have learned to undervalue relationships and instead prioritize protocols.[6] Most unfortunately, the church appears determined to follow secular examples: we discourage true vulnerability in relationships for the sake of maintaining appearance, we judge and condemn displayed or confessed imperfection, and correct "wrong-think" before being willing to listen. Like the secular world, the church prefers pamphlets, curricula, and techniques over the adventurous gamble found in genuine

6. Yalom, *Gift of Therapy*, 222–23.

relationships. This will continue to be a problem until our relationships fearlessly reflect the messages we are so fond of preaching. Again, despite this regression of relational understanding, the importance of relationship was once well understood. For instance, the birth of modern psychology can be traced to Josef Breuer's treatment of the infamous client Pappenheim. This patient was well-resourced and had received significant and numerous treatments from other professionals at the time. Breuer, however, took a different approach. In discussing Breuer's treatment of his most famous patient, Schwartz emphasized the importance that relationship played throughout the course of her care:

> Pappenheim's talking cure occurred in the context of her relationship with Breuer. Simple talking was not enough; the talking must be heard and must be felt to be heard. Pappenheim had been talking to her family in a language that frightened and confused them. It was only Breuer, because of his skill as a physician and his discipline as a scientist to be free of preconceptions, who was able to be present to hear her. Through his listening Breuer formed the necessary relationship with Pappenheim through which the talking cure could take place.[7]

We, in our own everyday fellowship, in our discipleship, in our families, and in our friendships, need to give more credit and emphasis to the depth of our relationships. We were created for relationships—with God *and* with others. To further this, God made relationship a necessary component of healing. The world does not *need* your advice, wisdom, expertise, tactics, or techniques; what is desperately needed is the miraculous and divine healing that is only available within sincere loving relationships.

> You shall love your neighbor as yourself.[8]

7. Schwartz, *Cassandra's Daughter*, 49.
8. Mark 12:31.

Questions to Ponder

1. Have you ever been in a discipleship relationship? If so, what was your experience?
2. What holds you back from fully engaging in a discipleship relationship?
3. Who could be your Paul? Who should be your Timothy?

Prayer

Lord,

I long to be close to you. I want to know you more. I want to grow in wisdom, knowledge, and understanding. I want to know better how to live in wisdom and pursue righteousness. Lord, lead me; I am your disciple. Send me, O God, someone to help me, to walk with me, to encourage me, to rebuke me, to help me grow. I pray for the courage to be vulnerable and teachable.

Amen.

CHAPTER 8

Our Calling

Recommended Reading: Acts, Gospel of Matthew

For many today, the church exists either for comfort or entertainment. Services are well rehearsed, uncontroversial, repetitive, benign, and, well, boring. Most churches filter through their content and time each component of spiritual engagement down to the minute as to ensure a gentle and subtle flow to the engagements of the morning. It begins with burnt coffee in the lobby and ends in overpriced lunch outings. And, for most Christians, this horrible summary is an accurate representation of the church experience. Some churches try harder than others to be a place of refuge, encouragement, and comfort to the downhearted; however, the reality for many of the beaten and bruised is that an hour on Sunday morning is fairly inconsequential when paired with an entire week of loneliness. Other churches spend exorbitant amounts on stage lights, fog machines, and professional performers whose hearts, we hope, are in the right place. These churches exist as entertainers; and, before you accuse me of being harshly judgmental, I do understand that their intention is to proclaim the name of Jesus while and through entertaining. But is this the heart of the church? Are these Sunday morning encounters all that we have to look forward to in our walk with Christ? I have been in many churches, and most churches talk about more. Unfortunately, very few churches live into more.

I want to live into more, and I know I'm not alone. I've had many conversations with Christians who know that they were called into an exciting adventure but are not quite sure how to begin. Others are waiting for permission.

The book of Acts is the story of the birth of the church, and it is a wild story. The apostles stepped into an adventure that definitely did not shy away from conflict or exist as entertainment for the masses. It begins with the ascension of Jesus, and the disciples staring into the sky.[1] Christ was no longer with them, and they stood there staring when they should have been moving their feet and getting their hands dirty. "Men of Galilee, why do you stand looking into heaven?"[2] When Jesus returns, as he has promised and foretold, it will be glorious and visible for all to see; until then, there's work to be done! Permission granted! Go! From that point forward, things started happening rapidly. As you read through Acts, you'll watch the disciples (students) become apostles (missionaries), you'll watch the formerly confused and naive disciples step forward with boldness and proclaim the gospel, you'll read about how the church spread across the Roman Empire like a wildfire, and you'll be witness to the movement and power of the Spirit poured out upon the church. Read Acts. The story is full of miracles, incredible generosity, murder, redemption, shipwrecks, betrayal . . . and, through it all, the Spirit of God moved. The church in the book of Acts is definitely not boring! And the Spirit that fell like fire upon the early church is the same Spirit that lives in you now. And the church is still moving; our story isn't over yet. Stop staring into the sky. Stop seeking to be entertained. Let's get messy. Let's get to work. We can comfort each other along the way, but our wild hearts will only ever truly find peace when we also find our place in the adventurous calling of God for his church. If you've ever, like many, like most men, felt that church

1. Acts 1:11.

2. Acts 1:11.

services were boring, then it's time to wake up, be filled with the Spirit, and start rattling some cages.

Baptism of the Holy Spirit

Jesus promised that we would not be left alone and that he would send a Helper, the Spirit of truth.[3] That promise is fulfilled after Christ's ascension on what we refer to as the day of Pentecost. Pentecost, which means "fiftieth" or "fiftieth day," was the Jewish festival of the harvest feast. It should not be considered a coincidence that the Spirit descended upon the believers in the upper room fifty days after Easter on what was being celebrated as a harvest festival; Jesus used the example of a harvest in his teachings and told us that the spiritual harvest was plentiful.

> And he said to them, "The harvest is plentiful, but the laborers are few. Therefore pray earnestly to the Lord of the harvest to send out laborers into his harvest."[4]

> And Jesus went throughout all the cities and villages, teaching in their synagogues and proclaiming the gospel of the kingdom and healing every disease and every affliction. When he saw the crowds, he had compassion for them, because they were harassed and helpless, like sheep without a shepherd. Then he said to his disciples, "The harvest is plentiful, but the laborers are few; therefore pray earnestly to the Lord of the harvest to send out laborers into his harvest."[5]

The believers were gathered together during a harvest celebration, they were continuing to obey Christ's instructions on the practice of communion, and, when the promise was fulfilled, the Holy Spirit came upon them like fire in a rushing wind.[6] They spoke in tongues and were able to preach the gospel to foreigners

3. Matt 28:20; John 15:26.
4. Luke 10:2.
5. Matt 9:35–38.
6. Acts 2:1–3.

in the languages of all the nations present.[7] They proclaimed the gospel with wisdom and boldness.[8] They healed the sick.[9] They cast out demons. They spoke and taught with authority. And the church grew.[10]

This power did not dissipate; rather, it grew. Despite even persecution, the church spread like a wildfire that could not be contained or suppressed. In fact, harsh persecution encouraged a large portion of the growth. We find this to be true today across the world. The more Christians are persecuted, the further the gospel spreads. Today, the same Spirit is our Helper. When we understand and embrace the power of the one that lives within us, when we recognize that we are filled with the Spirit of truth, the power of the gospel will pour out from us to a world desperate for good news; and nothing can contain the movement of the Spirit.

Many Parts, One Body

"Now you are the body of Christ and individual members of it."[11] Paul's words ring throughout the book of Acts. Individual members of the church went out into the world in unity with each other while serving through their unique gifts of the Spirit. They stood together in faithfulness to the message and mission of Christ.[12] They were unified as brothers and sisters, fathers and sons.[13] Acts shows that they held all things in common with each other, took care of each other, and recognized the need for each individual member. Paul's description of the physical body highlights the essential nature of each member of the church; in order to be whole,

7. Acts 2:4–13.

8. Acts 2:14–47.

9. Acts 3:1–10.

10. Acts 2:47.

11. 1 Cor 12:27.

12. Eph 4:5; 2 Cor 11:4.

13. Eph 6:23; Phil 4:21; 1 Tim 1:2; 1 Thess 5:25–26; 1 Pet 5:13; Rom 16:1–16; Acts 2:42–47, 4:32–35.

all must be present and engaged. This is essential; we, the global and local church, cannot do this without you.

There is nothing wrong or lowly about making the coffee for the church lobby in the morning. May God bless the works of your hands! In fact, God has a special place in his heart for those who practice even small displays of hospitality (truly, no act of hospitality should be considered "small"). But what would you do if you knew deep within your bones that you (yes, you!) were essential to the mission of Christ? What would you do if you knew with all your being that you were empowered in this essential mission by the Spirit of the Living God? Go and do it!

Also, there is life found in community. As stated before, we were created to be in relationship with each other; it is not good for us to be alone.[14] Consider also for a moment that we were created in a different manner than the rest of creation. In the beginning, God spoke creation into existence.[15] Nature was formed out of obedience to his command. However, when it came to us, God involved himself physically, artistically, and personally. He formed us, and breathed life into us;[16] through all of this, he made us in his image.[17] We were formed *within* relationship *for* relationship. Consider that in Hebrew the very word *life* only exists in the plural, and it has been well understood that the Hebraic perspective focused on life only truly existing within community and was not available in hermitage. We were made to meet with God as well as each other; this is why Buber remarks that "all real living is meeting."[18] It's worth stating, also, that how we meet with each other is a reflection of our relationship with God; when we hide our imperfections even from those closest to us, withhold sharing our struggles with those wanting to support us, feel embarrassed to share our opinions and perspectives with people who we call friends, lie about our current wellbeing to those who ask, and fear

14. Gen 2:18.

15. Gen 1:3, 6, 9, 11, 14, 20, 24.

16. Gen 2:7.

17. Gen 1:26–27.

18. Buber, *I and Thou*, 26.

retribution for displays of authenticity, we discover that our relationship with God is just as strained and disingenuous.

The Kingdom of Heaven Is Like . . .

The church is different. We are meant to be different. We are not to follow the example or path of the rest of the world. Unfortunately, we have a long history of wanting to be like everyone else. For more on that, read 1 Samuel in which the people of God specifically say, "That we also may be like all the nations."[19] God warned them then that there would be consequences to this request,[20] and they experienced those consequences for hundreds of years. We should heed the warning. The church is meant to be different.

A great example of just how different we are called to be can be found in the Gospel of Matthew. More than the others, Matthew recorded the teachings of Jesus with many of them beginning, "The kingdom of heaven is like . . ."[21] The parables depict a kingdom paradoxical to the secular world; if you want to read more about this, check out Donald Kraybill's *The Upside Down Kingdom*. More importantly, read the Gospel of Matthew.

> The kingdom of heaven is like a grain of mustard seed that a man took and sowed in his field. It is the smallest of all seeds, but when it has grown it is larger than all the garden plants and becomes a tree, so that the birds of the air come and make nests in its branches.[22]

This is a very curious parable. First, while mustard plants are resilient and have always been enjoyed as condiments (even in the ancient world), it has long been described (even to this day) as an invasive species. Mustard plants spread; and, because their seeds are so small and numerous, all attempts to remove this plant result in it spreading further and becoming even more

19. 1 Sam 8:20.
20. 1 Sam 8:10–18.
21. Matt 13:24, 31, 44, 45, 47.
22. Matt 13:31–32.

resilient. This invasive plant will not only consume your garden, but it will also crawl over your wall and dominate your neighbor's garden. It also, despite depictions in modern Christian art, does not grow into a mighty and glorious oak tree; it is more like a super-spreader weed. And the kind of birds that are attracted to bushes that only grow three to four feet high are not exactly the kinds of birds we enjoy seeing.

Does the parable make sense yet? We are not called, like an oak tree, to be a glorious beacon that brings attention to ourselves; we each are a small seed and are called to spread the good news of the kingdom of God; the glory of the church is found in the spreading of God's message. In so doing, we will be a welcomed refuge to the hurting, the rejected, the despised, the beat up, the burdened, the heartbroken, the weary, the sick, the lost, the sinners.

In this way, we should avoid imitating the secular world around us; in many ways, this can also include the supposed grand plans so many people dream of achieving. We can quickly lust after the large scale visions of the secular world at the expense of focusing on what truly matters most. Instead, be challenged to do small things, right things, godly things. According to the teachings of Jesus, this will yield an unstoppable crop. And isn't this the history of the church: twelve men traveled from place to place sharing the gospel and leading others to follow Christ. The more the church was persecuted, the faster and further it spread to the lost and hurting poor of the world. Within their lifetime, they witnessed the church start in a small room on Pentecost and spread until it consumed the entire Roman Empire and beyond.

The Great Commission

The church has been commissioned, and this means you! You have been commissioned, deployed, charged, appointed, commanded, employed, mandated, entrusted.

> All authority in heaven and on earth has been given to me. Go therefore and make disciples of all nations, baptizing them in the name of the Father and of the Son

> and of the Holy Spirit, teaching them to observe all that I have commanded you. And behold, I am with you always, to the end of the age.[23]

Go and make disciples. Evangelism is not an activity for some members of the church. Jesus tells us that we are, whether or not we choose to be, the salt and light of the earth.[24] Sharing the gospel is not reserved for those who are particularly skilled in the art of conversation, or those who enjoy talking to strangers, or those who enjoy meeting new people. Sharing the good news of the gospel of Christ *is* the mission of the church, and it is for all of us.

23. Matt 28:18–20.
24. Matt 5:13–14.

Questions to Ponder

1. Have you recognized the presence of the Holy Spirit in your life? Have you accepted that you have been filled with the Spirit? What does that look like?
2. How can you further live into the truth that you, as a follower of Christ, are filled with the Holy Spirit?
3. What first steps can you take to "go and make disciples"?
4. How can you be more engaged and involved in church?

Prayer

God,

I know you have not called me to live alone; you have graced me not only with your Spirit, but also with a fellowship of believers. You are great and gracious, and I pray that you will continue to empower me to share of your goodness. Help me, Father, to be fully present and available to my brothers and sisters in you. Show me how I can further be deployed as your ambassador, and give me the opportunity to share the gospel and make disciples. I pray, LORD, *for your church. I pray that you will embolden her. I pray that your Spirit will be felt; may the presence of your Spirit be experienced by the believers for your glory. Let us not be found staring into the sky but rather as workers of the harvest, as fishers or men.*

Amen.

CHAPTER 9

The Heart of God

Recommended Reading: Jonah

The book of Jonah is an amazing story that most of us know, but it's always surprising to find out how many of us have not read this short book in its entirety. Within this short account, we typically have discussions centered on disobedience and repentance; Jonah disobeyed the command of God and instead fled in the opposite direction—he was later repentant of his disobedience, but there wasn't much of a change of heart. Further investigation of Jonah should start a discussion on the topic of anger; God asks Jonah the same question twice regarding Jonah's reaction to his circumstances: "Is it right for you to be angry?"[1] However, have you ever considered the book of Jonah to be a conversation about evangelism? Read through Jonah (it's only four chapters) and consider the message given about the amazing heart of God.

1. Jonah 4:4.

The Heart of God

The story of Jonah begins with God giving the command for Jonah to go and give a message of repentance: "Go to Nineveh, that great city, and call out against it, for their evil has come up before me."[2] Nineveh was the capital city of the Assyrian Empire with a population estimated to be approximately two million people located in what is now modern day Mosul, Iraq. The story begins with God seeing the state of the people, knowing the wickedness, and choosing to first send a messenger. God wanted to see the people repentant and renewed; his heart was broken for the city, and he delayed wrath and judgment to first offer the hope of salvation.

God has a heart for the lost. And this is precisely why Jonah disobeyed. Jonah provides the explanation for his anger and disobedience:

> He prayed to the LORD and said, "O LORD is not this what I said when I was yet in my country? That is why I made haste to flee to Tarshish; for I knew that you are a gracious God and merciful, slow to anger, and abounding in steadfast love, and relenting from disaster."[3]

Evangelism begins with understanding that the heart of God is abounding in steadfast love for the wicked with the desire that all would turn to him. So, this leads to a basic question: Why did Jonah find this to be a problem? Before we begin criticizing Jonah too harshly, we must first take a look at the historical context; we have to understand who the Ninevites were.

Jonah Running

Jonah's disobedient response to the command of God is, unfortunately, relatable. The Assyrians were a ruthless people who waged a merciless and horrific war against the Northern Kingdom of Israel; and Jonah spent his life with a front row seat. At the hand of raiding

2. Jonah 1:2.
3. Jonah 4:2.

armies, Israeli children were slaughtered and pregnant woman were cut open. The Assyrians were known less for governance and more for pillage and burn. To these people Jonah was commanded to be the messenger for a merciful God who is abounding in steadfast love who relents from punishment. To these people, Jonah was called to preach salvation. And Jonah was sent to their capital.

When reading through Jonah, be careful to not judge the Ninevites. First, we must read this story knowing that we *are* the Ninevites; we are wretched sinners deserving of wrath but instead receive the grace of God. If we are a new creation in Christ Jesus, then let us remember that we were once something else and are now redeemed by the blood of Christ. Evangelism, then, requires knowing the message of salvation because we *are* the saved. In truth, our world is filled with two types of people. On the one hand, there are the obvious *problems*. The problem category is filled with the liars, the narcissists, the apathetic, the corrupt, the inconsiderate, the inhumane, the unrepentant, and the like. On the other hand are those who foolishly believe they do not belong to the *problem* category.

Second, we need to recognize the difficulties we have in going as missionaries to certain people. Jonah's desire to avoid giving a message of hope to the Ninevites ought to be expected; we would have done the same and probably are doing the same right now. We all have been wronged. We all have experienced hardship and conflict. And, partly because of this, we all also have tendencies toward judgment of others. When reading Jonah, listen intently for the compassionate heart of God. He sees the wickedness of Nineveh, but he loves them, and he wants his prodigal children to come home. Of all the wonders of God, of all that thrills and amazes, of all that confuses and frustrates, of all the questions that our minds cannot fathom, what many of us struggle with most is the nature of grace itself. Grace welcomes and forgives no matter the cost; it actively seeks out the lost and pursues the unworthy. Grace is the Father's greatest gift as well as his most counterintuitive mystery. And this, grace itself, is the problem. It's Jonah's problem, and, if we're honest, it's our problem too.

Many brilliant writers have sought to describe the boundless grace of God by poetically and vividly painting glorious portrayals of the ferocity of the Father's love and depth of his Son's compassion. But if we take the time to thoroughly reflect, our conclusion should be that we have boundaries and grace does not. It appears rational to us according to our understanding to withhold grace to those deemed undeserving—the repeat offender, the arrogant, the unrepentant—while instead lavishing it upon those determined to have made valiant attempts. But the Father has a history of moving towards those who would defy his name and mock his crown. Is this not the story of the Ninevites in the book of Jonah? Is this not the parable of the prodigal son?[4] Or even the story of the apostle Paul—no one mocked the name of Jesus or persecuted his followers more ardently than the man who would later encounter Jesus on the Damascus road.[5] Paul would not only find grace and compassion but would also become an essential church leader and the one who wrote the most about grace. What would you do if you discovered that your church pastor had a very recent past like Paul's? The God of boundless grace demonstrates his love not by meeting our expectations of rational behavior but rather by pursuing the resistant and melting the heart of stone. When called to bring a message of grace and hope to an undeserving people, Jonah decided for himself that the grace of God was foolishness; he ran not from a god of vengeance and retribution, but from the God of ferocious love and boundless grace. He ran because he knew that God would allow for the possibility of redemption and renovation.[6] We should recognize that we are Jonah running.

It's Not About You

The next lesson we can learn about evangelism through Jonah is simple: it's not about you. The job of the prophet was to give

4. Luke 15:11–32.
5. Acts 9:1–19.
6. Jonah 4:2.

God's message primarily to the king but also to the people. In this way, Jonah was extremely successful. Jonah was sent to the most evil city in the world (at least at the time) and the result was repentance at all levels; a city with a population of approximately two million turned to God—everyone from the king down to even the livestock. However, after giving God's message of pending destruction due to their wickedness (not exactly a message graciously given), Jonah found a comfortable place to sit so he could enjoy watching their doom. It appears safe to say that Jonah's heart and attitude were not the best examples for us to follow. He preached with anger and a desire to watch them be destroyed. Repentance was not his goal; Jonah was hoping for their destruction. And yet, the people responded. Why? Because it was not about Jonah; it never was. It was always about God. Jonah reluctantly obeyed, and God moved. Jonah did not preach a message reflective of the love of God, but still the people responded. The people responded because God moved.

We need to stop perpetuating the excuse (the lie) that some will not be effective as an evangelist because they are not eloquent or scholarly. If you think that such a description applies to you, here's some good news: it's not about you.

Come and See

Another highly successful biblical evangelist who perhaps is a better role model in both approach and attitude is the woman at the well.[7] This woman had a life-changing encounter with Jesus that transformed her life. She then ran through the town (through the crowds of people who rejected her and left her to live in shame) and shared her experience. She didn't spend time arguing or convincing. She did not utilize the Socratic method of debate to intellectually prove her perspective. She wasn't eloquent or sophisticated. In fact, her approach did not uplift or glorify herself at all; instead, she gave a simple invitation: "Come, see a

7. John 4:1–30.

man."[8] The woman at the well gives us the example of not sharing *what* you know, but rather sharing *who* you know. But what is also remarkable about this woman is the vulnerability she was willing to display. She not only did not glorify herself, she also did not attempt to present herself as a worthy advocate. Rather, she joyfully announced that the shame which once afflicted her was not central to her understanding of salvation. Her message to the people who once shamed her existence was an invitation for them to "see a man who told me all that I ever did."[9] She did not share with them only the seemingly acceptable imperfections; she was vulnerable, transparent, and beautifully raptured by graced.

Now It's Your Turn

You are called to share the gospel. The command to Jonah, the order to "get up and go,"[10] is not limited to Jonah. While there are some who are gifted with evangelism, those to whom evangelism comes easily, particularly gifted or not, you are called. And why wouldn't you share *who* you know? When you've encountered Jesus, like the woman at the well, that experience cannot be contained! Share about the one you've encountered, remembering that Jesus taught us that "the harvest is plentiful but the workers are few."[11] You, as a disciple of Christ, are called to be his ambassador.[12] It's your turn. Get up and go.

8. John 4:29.
9. John 4:29.
10. Jonah 1:2.
11. Luke 10:2.
12. 2 Cor 5:20.

Questions to Ponder

1. What opportunities do you have in your current daily routine to share Jesus?
2. When thinking about sharing the good news of Christ, who comes to mind? When will you see them next?
3. What holds you back from evangelism and how can you overcome it?
4. Is there anyone in your life you are struggling to forgive? Who is your "Nineveh"?

Prayer

Father,

Give me a heart for the lost. Thank you for the grace and compassion that you have showed me; thank you for redeeming me. Thank you for your sacrifice on the cross and for the redeeming blood of Christ. I pray that you guide me to opportunities to share my testimony, to share of my encounters with you. Lead me, Father. Send me. And give me the courage to go.

Amen.

CHAPTER 10

The Savior of the World

Recommended Reading: Hebrews

Let's deviate for a moment to a short history lesson.

Pax Romana

After returning from a successful campaign, General Octavian, one of the great leaders of the Gallic Wars (Rome's conquest of Europe), turned his passions to political aspirations. His rival, Marc Antony, was the prodigy of Julius Caesar and was held in high esteem among the Roman people—his new relationship and collaboration with Julius Caesar's former lover, Cleopatra (the powerful, beautiful, and beloved leader of Egypt), helped his image and popularity. But Octavian was brilliant and relentless; he successfully seized all political power in Rome, defeated the campaign and aspirations of Marc Antony, and followed in the footsteps of Julius Caesar. Like Julius Caesar, Octavian did not want to be viewed as having the likeness of Mars (the god of war); he wanted to be worshiped and revered as a true god. He began using the name Augustus and spoke of himself as being a deity for whom the entire world should be grateful. The imperial calendar was even re-organized to center on the birth of this god, this Caesar. His story was written on the calendar so that all may know of his miraculous deeds; in this writing, Augustus was described as the divine Caesar being equal to the beginning of all things for having restored stability. His birthday stood as a signal for the beginning of life and real living, the end of regret, and the promise of blessing.[1] Augustus was said to be the savior who adorned his people with peace and the highest good while exceeding the expectations of all who waited with anticipation for the gospel, the good news.[2]

Pax Romana (Roman Peace) is a topic that has been discussed by many historians for years. It is said to be an era of Roman history covering over two hundred years that started with Caesar Augustus. Despite all that has been said, Pax Romana was a lie. Most within the Roman Empire, approximately 90 percent, lived as peasants.[3] During those two hundred years, Rome only had a few in which it was not in an active state of war. Rome also infamously ruled the world with an iron fist and crucified any that stood in opposition to its power. Because Romans were master architects and engineers, and because a strong infrastructure (primarily for trade and military purposes) was a priority of Rome, all roads really did lead to Rome; and, after a rebellion, miles and miles of these roads would be lined with crucified traitors as a message to all entering the empire: "This is what happens to those who threaten our power." But, like all clever politicians, Augustus promised through his marketing to be a man of the people who brought peace to the lowly.

Meanwhile, in the Gospel of Luke, we read,

> In those days a decree went out from Caesar Augustus that all the world should be registered. . . .
>
> There were shepherds out in the field, keeping watch over their flock by night. And an angel of the Lord appeared to them, and the glory of the Lord shone around

1. Danker, *Benefactor*, 216.
2. Danker, *Benefactor*, 217.
3. Carter, *Matthew and Empire*, 19.

> them, and they were filled with great fear. And the angel said to them, "Fear not, for behold, I bring you good news of great joy that will be for all the people. For unto you is born this day in the city of David a Savior, who is Christ the Lord. And this will be a sign for you: you will find a baby wrapped in swaddling cloths and lying in a manger." And suddenly there was with the angel a multitude of the heavenly host praising God and saying, "Glory to God in the highest, and on earth peace among those with whom he is pleased."[4]

The angels appear to real shepherds and not to a politician pretending to be a shepherd. And, as they did so, they proclaimed a message of peace that would truly be for all people—starting with the lowly. Augustus started a lie through the entire empire about Roman peace, but the angels brought a contradictory message. Peace would not come from Rome. Peace would come from God through his salvation. Augustus may claim the title of savior of the world, and many were fooled—are still fooled. Marc Antony was defeated and Augustus assumed all political power; but, despite the title Caesar (Latin word for the ruling political authority, the dictator king), only Jesus would truly be Christ (Greek word for the anointed one, the chosen one, the king).

The world promises us much. The world promises us happiness, fulfillment, excitement, love, peace, prosperity. But as Proverbs warns us, for all those tricked into following these hollow promises, they will unfortunately discover that the road leads only to death and decay.[5] I implore you. Hear the message of the angels: available to you is the true savior of the world, Christ the LORD, and with him comes the lasting peace of God.

Because of the false promises of the world, we need to maintain a clear and biblical understanding of who Jesus is; even in the times of the apostles, many arose as teachers presenting false gospels twisting the teachings of Jesus. The apostles responded in their letters to various churches with strict warnings and

4. Luke 2:1, 8–14.

5. Prov 9:18.

compassionate guidance to return to the true Christ. The most direct teaching in the New Testament on the identity of Christ can be found in the book of Hebrews. While reading Hebrews, hold fast to Jesus and remain in awe of our savior.

We must not stray from who Jesus is.

The Lord, God, and Savior

There is no salvation apart from Jesus. The world tells us otherwise, but we must know the truth. "We have been sanctified through the offering of the body of Jesus Christ once for all."[6] His sacrifice was sufficient, and nothing else will do. He is the one source of our salvation[7] and the great high priest[8] who offers a more excellent covenant.[9] When angels proclaimed the good news of God, the gospel, to the shepherds, they were not making an announcement about a coming message or teaching—they were announcing the arrival of Jesus.

> I bring you good news of great joy that will be for all the people. For unto you is born this day in the city of David a Savior, who is Christ the Lord.[10]

Jesus does not bring the good news; he *is* the good news. In that regard, we cannot be without hope for he is our hope. In our striving and struggling, we do not hope *for*, we hope *in*. Hope and love remain,[11] always with us, always available, because Jesus has promised to always be with us.[12]

Likewise, Jesus was not a man who was granted authority in heaven for his deeds. Jesus *is* God. The author of Hebrews tells

6. Heb 10:10.
7. Heb 2:11.
8. Heb 4:14.
9. Heb 8:6.
10. Luke 2:10–11.
11. 1 Cor 13:13.
12. Matt 28:20.

us, "Jesus Christ is the same yesterday and today and forever."[13] This is an echo from the prophet Malachi: "For I the LORD do not change."[14] The apostle John started his gospel account with this truth: "In the beginning was the Word, and the Word was with God, and the Word was God."[15] To believe in the Holy Trinity (God the Father, Jesus the Son, and the Holy Spirit) is not to believe in a plurality; we believe in one God who presents himself to us in three separate forms. Jesus is God in the flesh.[16] This is why we worship him; this is why we pray to and worship Jesus. In his name there is power.

Because of this, it is not enough to call upon Jesus to save us; we must also call him LORD. And making him lord of our lives means that he is in charge. The book of Hebrews tells us that Jesus is supreme,[17] greater than all who came before,[18] the founder and perfecter of our faith,[19] and king of a kingdom that cannot be shaken.[20] There are other religions that acknowledge Jesus as being important, good, and wise, but where we differ is in our knowledge of the supremacy of Christ.

Consider for a moment that making Jesus ruler of our lives, calling him LORD, is to be taken into context with the Ten Commandments. The first three read,

> You shall have no other gods before me. You shall not make for yourself a carved image, or any likeness of anything that is in heaven above, or that is in the earth beneath, or that is in the water under the earth. You shall not bow down to them or serve them, for I the LORD

13. Heb 13:8.
14. Mal 3:6.
15. John 1:1.
16. John 1:14.
17. Heb 1:1–14.
18. Heb 3:1–6.
19. Heb 12:1–2.
20. Heb 12:18–29.

> your God am a jealous God. . . . You shall not take the name of the LORD your God in vain.[21]

Jesus is not simply important or wise; he is not simply a good teacher or a positive role model. He was not a loving man who cared for his people. Jesus is supreme; there is no other name to rival his.[22] He is the Alpha and Omega, the beginning and the end.[23] Nothing was created except through the power and will of Jesus.[24]

The Wounded Christ

Jesus asked his disciples directly who he was to them; Peter's answer was as direct as ours needs to be. And, as we read through Hebrews, we will learn what we need to answer with Peter's confidence.

> "But who do you say that I am?"
>
> Simon Peter replied, "You are the Christ, the Son of the living God."[25]

As Christians, we need to know who Jesus really is; I cannot say that enough. There have been and will continue to be many who make claims about Christ, but if we turn to Scripture, we will find the truth. Jesus is the Christ, the Anointed One. And the description of what that means is not mysterious; read through Hebrews to improve your understanding. Jesus is the Son of God, the one anointed by God to save humanity from our sins. But he did not come as expected; despite his right to it, he did not come to claim worldly power or position. Instead, he came to die.

He kept his scars. Christians, rightfully so, often speak of the sacrifice of Christ: his death and resurrection. But rarely, if ever, do you hear the truth that he kept his scars. Honestly, nowhere in

21. Exod 20:3–7.
22. Phil 2:9.
23. Rev 22:13.
24. John 1:3.
25. Matt 16:15–16; Luke 9:20.

history have any considered such a ridiculous, counterintuitive character as the God we serve; he continues to baffle our wisdom and silence our understanding. Consider for a moment the weight of such a thought as a God who weeps, suffers, mourns—a God with scars. Common mythologies speak of gods and goddesses of beauty, strength, power, and, most importantly, worldly perfection; they display a majestic glow as they walk upon the heavenly realms. The realm of the gods was reserved for the powerful royal elite and offered little, if any, comfort to the peasants and serfs in desperate need of their attention—while the desperate were ignored, the elite were validated in actions of slavery, oppression, and conquest. Stories of such gods and goddesses exist out of the reason and rationale of the human psyche; rulers were adorned with gold and rubies upon glorious high seats of power and splendor. The scars of Christ stand in direct opposition to common wisdom and reason.

The biblical narrative challenges historical definitions of beauty, strength, and splendor by introducing a God who consistently chooses to operate in extremes to cultural understanding. In regard to beauty, if kings are to be born with the elite, and if priests are to be conceived of those considered socially righteous and influential, Christ's birth stands in opposition to understanding. Born of a mother of poor stature from a rejected community who was naively considered to have acted impurely outside of the bond of marriage, to a poor father who almost sought divorce from his presumed adulterous wife, and even amongst the company of livestock, the nativity story strives to bring hope not to elite but to the lowest of shepherds watching over the flocks by night.[26] The beauty of Christ, then, relies not upon his grandeur but upon his humility. The beauty found in the nativity does not rely solely upon the message presented but rather offers a new concept: God made poor. The very name presented, Emmanuel, essential to the nativity message, means *God with us*. Christ does not identify with or understand the poor—he is poor; through Christ, the God of creation becomes meek. In regard to strength, the people of God were

26. Luke 2:8.

chosen not for their influence and elegance but for their complete lack of both; the prophet Ezekiel offers the description of God's selection of the Israelites by comparing them to an unwanted infant abandoned in the wilderness where "no one looked on [them] with pity."[27] It was through these social rejects that God planned to revealed his power and grace; the omnipotent chose the weak. To display splendor, the God of heaven chose not to rest upon a throne amongst royalty but upon a cross with the guilty.[28]

The truth of God's word, then, always penetrates and convicts because it requires of us the courage to change everything; it demands a shift in our perspective. Even the resurrection offers revolutionary theology. Often, we rejoice in the one "who . . . made himself nothing, taking the very nature of a servant."[29] We rejoice because that is not the end of the story; because of such an act, "God exalted him to the highest place."[30] Christ offered himself as a sacrifice for our transgressions, and, because of this act of self-sacrifice, the Father adorned his Son with "all authority in heaven and on earth."[31] But with his glorification, the initial four words grow in mystery and power: Christ kept his scars. His ascent to glory did not erase the pain, sorrow, and humility. Nicholas Wolterstorff wrote,

> The wounds of Christ are his identity. They tell us who he is. He did not lose them. They went down into the grave with him and they came up with him—visible, tangible, palpable. Rising did not remove them. He who broke the bonds of death kept his wounds.[32]

Perhaps the rising and glorification of Christ are different than we have ever imagined. Maybe his ascent is less elegant and royal than we would prefer. Maybe that's the point.

27. Ezek 16:5.
28. Luke 23:32–33.
29. Phil 2:6–7.
30. Phil 2:9.
31. Matt 28:18.
32. Wolterstorff, *Lament for a Son*, 92.

"Then he said to Thomas, 'Put your finger here, and see my hands; and put out your hand, and place it in my side.'"[33] The glory of the resurrected stills hungers, thirsts, bleeds. Not only did Christ return from the grave with scars, but those scars also never healed. His appearance before Thomas allowed the disciples to touch the wounds that were as fresh as the day they were received; it were as if Christ took pleasure in the marks. What if we serve a God that rejoices in the scars he bears? What if the scars are not a sign of his suffering but of his triumph? Even in Revelation, as we are given a depiction of the glorious return of Christ, we are given a description of the King of kings descending in triumph which includes the detail that he is wearing a blood stained robe.[34] "By his stripes we are healed,"[35] and Christ stands proud to bear those marks for eternity. We serve a God that is regularly challenging and redefining our understanding of triumph, victory, and glory; he calls—entices—us into a world in which "if anyone would be first, he must be last of all and servant of all."[36] Our God, then, does not hide or ignore the physical marks of shame, the wounds of the crucifixion; rather, the marks are emphasized and displayed. He keeps the scars of his sacrifice not out of a call to pity or mourning but as a badge of honor. With his last breath, he does not cry out "it is finished"[37] as a sigh of relief that the anguish is over, but as an acknowledgement that he has finally fulfilled what he has pursued since the garden. Christianity relies on the paradox of the cross: through crucifixion, Christ is victorious. We serve a God that takes pride in the scars he bears. We serve a God that upgraded a crown of gold and a heavenly throne for a crown of thorns and the glory of the cross. In my own speculations, I have often wondered if, when I finally arrive, I will be greeted by my savior and king proudly adorned with his thorny crown.

33. John 20:27.

34. Rev 19:13.

35. Isa 53:5.

36. Mark 9:35.

37. John 19:30.

The biblical narrative tells the story of a God who chooses to identify with the weak, the burdened, the neglected, the poor. He is the omnipotent that does not attach his name to the powerful or influential, but rather to the arguably incompetent and incapable. This alone would be enough to radically rewrite humanity's concept of strength and power, but God, again, challenges conventional wisdom by displaying solidarity with his people. He does not join the meek; he becomes meek. God's common declaration—"You will be my people, and I will be your God"[38]—becomes anything but common through the lenses of God's radical solidarity.

If God's people are dirty, he is dirty. If they hunger, he hungers. If they weep, he weeps. Buber, in a debate with a friend about God, wrote about his desire to hold tightly to the Name that stands with humanity in the loneliest darkness. "Is it not He who *hears* them?"[39] David sang about the beauty of God by declaring that the "poor man cried, and the LORD heard him."[40] And, as a beautiful picture of the heart of God, we learn through David's song that "the LORD is near to the brokenhearted."[41]

Gutierrez once wrote that "the Son of God teaches us that talk of God must be mediated by the experience of the cross. He accepts abandonment and death precisely in order to reveal God to us as love."[42] He generally argues that to gain solidarity with the poor, hungry, and suffering is to better your understanding of God himself. Walter Brueggemann writes that God "sits in the divine council on the edge of his seat and is attentive to his special interests."[43] God is active and does not refrain from interacting with history and joining his beloveds in their suffering; he is alert, engaged, and unwilling to leave us abandoned. Nicholas Wolterstorff considers a God who "sent his beloved son to suffer *like* us," who "instead of explaining our suffering . . . shares it,"

38. Gen 17:7; Exod 6:7; Ezek 34:24, 36:28; Jer 7:23, 30:22, 31:33.

39. Buber, *Eclipse of God*, 18.

40. Ps 34:6.

41. Ps 34:18.

42. Gutierrez, *On Job*, 97.

43. Brueggemann, *Prophetic Imagination*, 15.

whose sorrow is so great none can look upon it, and who rescued us from our suffering by becoming the suffering servant.[44] God takes pride in his crown of thorns. Maybe the words "God, make me more like you," are far more dangerous and radical than we can fathom. Maybe they are words we do not or cannot understand. Maybe they are words we should fear. What would it mean to earnestly seek God's heart with all that we have if our understanding of God became humbler, dirtier, maybe even culturally appalling? What if we sought the active God who does not sit on the sidelines, the God who hungers, the God of immense sorrow, the God who mourns, the God who dwells not amongst the influential and rich in houses of luxury and status but joyfully sits in the gutters of the slums with the truly meek? Would we recognize this God? Would we want to?

The prophet Jeremiah offers consolation to the poor in spirit when he announces the grace of God to a weeping nation. The comfort comes in the form a letter, the words of God, delivered to the seemingly rejected, despised, and forgotten—a letter written to those exiled in Babylon. He writes that the heart of God can be found when earnestly and fervently sought: "You will seek me and find me, when you seek me with all your heart. I will be found by you."[45] In consideration of God's timeless attempt to challenge our views, the *seeking* arguably becomes a shift in perspective rather than righteous adherence to ritualistic principles and practices. Rather than doctrinally upholding the man-made pillars of faithful religion, the whispers of God allure us back into the wanderings, the day-by-day ventures, through the wilderness.[46] Christ beckons us to not become religious elitists but to follow him. Finding God does not rely upon adherence to religious rules and regulations but upon a heart that is vulnerable enough to grasp the beauty and splendor of the least.

44. Wolterstorff, *Lament for a Son*, 81. Emphasis original.

45. Jer 29:13–14.

46. Hos 2:14.

Questions to Ponder

1. In what ways are you still looking to the world to bring you peace?
2. What is different between the peace of the world and the peace of God?
3. What does it mean to make Jesus Lord of your life?

Prayer

Jesus,

You are L*ORD* *over all; you reign over heaven and earth. Blessed be your name! I praise you, Jesus, for you are great and in your name is power. Thank you that I may hold onto your promises, that you are the same yesterday, today, and tomorrow. Forgive me, Jesus, for my wanderings, for not always keeping you as my Lord. Forgive me, Jesus, and hold me close that I ever more follow you. I love you, Jesus. Lead me. Help me.*

Amen.

CHAPTER 11

Afterword

Recommended Reading: John 15

Abide in my love.[1]

Abide in me.[2]

If you hear nothing else, please hear this. Let this word sink deep into your heart: abide. The word means "to remain" or "to make your home." Apart from Christ, we will wither; but when we are connected to him, when we are connected to the vine,[3] we will produce amazing fruit.[4] Through Christ, the labors of our efforts will be nourishing to those around us, and we will be fragrant and sweet to the world around us. This is not because of us or our efforts, but only because of Christ, only because we are connected to him.

Beyond our efforts for productive labor, there is nothing like (and no way to describe) what it is like to make your home in Christ. This *is* the experience we will have for eternity in heaven;

1. John 15:9.
2. John 15:4.
3. John 15:5.
4. John 15:5.

and we can start now. Heaven on earth *is* remaining in union with Jesus.

> Now Moses used to take the tent and pitch it outside the camp, far off from the camp, and he called it the tent of meeting. And everyone who sought the LORD would go out to the tent of meeting, which was outside the camp. Whenever Moses went out to the tent, all the people would rise up, and each would stand at his tent door, and watch Moses until he had gone into the tent. When Moses entered the tent, the pillar of cloud would descend and stand at the entrance of the tent, and the LORD would speak with Moses. And when all the people saw the pillar of cloud standing at the entrance of the tent, all the people would rise up and worship, each at his tent door. Thus the LORD used to speak to Moses face to face, as a man speaks to his friend. When Moses turned again into the camp, his assistant Joshua the son of Nun, a young man, would not depart from the tent.[5]

Meet with God, I beg you. Meet with God. The Lord wants to speak to you, he longs to speak with you, he has made himself available to you, face to face as a friend. Meet with God, then remain. Meet with God, then refuse to depart from his presence.

> *Abide in my love.*[6]

5. Exod 33:7–11.
6. John 15:9. Emphasis added.

Bibliography

Augustine. *Confessions*. Translated by R. S. Pine-Coffin. London: Penguin Group, 1961.

Browning, Christopher R. *Ordinary Men: Reserve Police Battalion 101 and the Final Solution in Poland*. New York: HarperCollins, 1992.

Brueggemann, Walter. *The Prophetic Imagination*. 2nd ed. Minneapolis: Fortress, 2001.

Buber, Martin. *Eclipse of God: Studies in the Relation Between Religion and Philosophy*. New York: Harper and Brothers, 1952.

———. *I and Thou*. New York: Scribner Classics, 1958.

Carter, Warren. *Matthew and Empire: Initial Explorations*. Harrisburg, PA: Trinity, 2001.

Danker, Frederick W. *Benefactor: An Epigraphic Study of Graeco-Roman and New Testament Semantic Field*. St. Louis: Clayton, 1982.

Eldredge, John. *Wild at Heart: Discovering the Secret of a Man's Soul*. Nashville: Thomas Nelson, 2001.

Frankl, Viktor E. *Man's Search for Meaning*. Boston: Beacon, 1959.

Freeman, John. "Face to Face: Carl Gustav Jung (1959)." KidMillions, Oct. 10, 2017. YouTube video. https://www.youtube.com/watch?v=2AMu-G51yTY.

Goggin, Jamin, and Kyle Strobel. *Beloved Dust: Drawing Close to God by Discovering the Truth About Yourself*. Nashville: Nelson, 2014.

Gutierrez, Gustavo. *On Job: God-Talk and the Suffering of the Innocent*. New York: Orbis, 1987.

Kierkegaard, Søren. *Works of Love*. New York: First Harper Torchbook, 1962.

Kopp, Herb. *A Gospel for a New People: Studies in the Sermon on the Mount*. Winnipeg: Kindred Productions, 2003.

Kraybill, Donald B. *The Upside Down Kingdom*. Scottsdale, PA: Herald, 1978.

Lewis, C. S. *The Complete Chronicles of Narnia*. London: Collins, 2000.

———. *Till We Have Faces: A Myth Retold*. Orlando: Harcourt, 1956.

Manning, Brennan. *Abba's Child: The Cry of the Heart for Intimate Belonging.* Colorado Springs: NavPress, 1994.

———. *The Furious Longing of God.* Colorado Springs: David C. Cook, 2009.

———. *The Ragamuffin Gospel.* Colorado Springs: Multnomah, 2005.

———. *The Relentless Tenderness of Jesus.* Grand Rapids: Revell, 2004.

Newman, James. "Socialist Realism: Stalin's Control of Art in the Soviet Union." *The Collector*, Sept. 12, 2021. https://www.thecollector.com/soviet-realism-stalin-control/.

Sauytbay, Sayragul, and Alexandra Cavelius. *The Chief Witness: Escape from China's Modern-Day Concentration Camps.* Translated by Caroline Waight. London: Scribe, 2021.

Schwartz, Joseph. *Cassandra's Daughter: A History of Psychoanalysis.* New York: Penguin Group, 1999.

Shakespeare, William. *The Merchant of Venice.* In *The Complete Works of William Shakespeare*, edited by W. G. Clark and W. Aldis Wright, 331–55. New York: Nelson Doubleday, 1950.

———. "Sonnet 94." In *The Oxford Book of English Verse*, edited by Christopher Ricks, 83–84. New York: Oxford University Press, 1999.

Solzhenitsyn, Aleksandr. *The Gulag Archipelago 1918–1956: An Experiment in Literary Investigation.* Translated by Thomas P. Whitney and Harry Willets. Abridged by Edward E. Ericsson Jr. London: Harvill, 1986.

Stassen, Glen H. *Living the Sermon on the Mount: A Practical Hope for Grace and Deliverance.* San Francisco: Jossey-Bass, 2006.

Taylor, John H., ed. *Journey Through the Afterlife: Ancient Egyptian Book of the Dead.* Cambridge: Harvard University Press, 2010.

Wolterstorff, Nicholas. *Lament for a Son.* Grand Rapids: Eerdmans, 1987.

Woodcrest Chapel. "Brennan Manning—Did You Believe That I Loved You?" Core Bible Study, Mar. 26, 2017. YouTube video. https://www.youtube.com/watch?v=4AehcGSIkZw.

Yalom, Irving, D. *The Gift of Therapy: An Open Letter to a New Generation of Therapists and Their Patients.* New York: HarperCollins, 2002.

Yancey, Philip. "God, the Jilted Lover." *Christianity Today* 30:8 (May 1986) 72. https://www.christianitytoday.com/1986/05/god-jilted-lover-2/.

———. *The Jesus I Never Knew.* Grand Rapids: Zondervan, 1995.

www.ingramcontent.com/pod-product-compliance
Lightning Source LLC
Chambersburg PA
CBHW071057090426
42737CB00013B/2360

9798385233854